POST
ON BICYCLES

Taking Command of English Language

By

FRANCES McKIE

ACKNOWLEDGEMENT

To Jan Morris for permission to include her article,
"Oil on Granite".

I would like to thank Andrew Easton, Anne Mackay
and Fraser Sutherland who kindly helped me to
complete this book.

CONTENTS

FOREWORD

Robert Henry Robins, Emeritus Professor of General Linguistics, University of London, and David Crystal, Honorary Professor of Linguistics, Bangor University, define language as "a system of conventional spoken, manual, or written symbols by means of which human beings, as members of a social group and participants in its culture, express themselves. The functions of language include communication, the expression of identity, play, imaginative expression, and emotional release."

Language is indeed a chief means by which society functions and it is therefore essential that each individual is able to acquire not only the basic elements of the language but is also able to employ its more sophisticated forms in order to be an empowered member of society.

In this age of mass media, where spin-doctors, politicians, press barons, news channels, advertisers - each with their own agenda - increasingly employ the arts of manipulative rhetoric to influence public opinion, it is even more urgent to empower the individual with the skills to analyse such communications, closely.

Such manipulators frequently avoid the detailed, reasoned argument which the English language can convey and turn instead to devices such as bold headlines, slogans, mantras and sound bites, knowing full well that more and more people, coping with the demands of everyday life, are less likely to examine and weigh up the 'message' in order to determine what is actually true, what is propaganda or what is hard sell.

Significantly, Eton College, on its website, 'EtonX', warns that "our world is changing fast and in order to get ahead, students need the soft skills, practical skills and entrepreneurial mindset that are essential for success in life." For £350, the college is offering teenagers a course called 'Making an Impact' which will help them to get their "ideas and opinions heard and develop influencing skills to increase leadership capabilities." They will learn to "understand and implement different techniques to influence and persuade others."

In a social climate where the proliferation of disinformation and the manipulation of populations continues to spread, it is even more essential to teach how to distinguish between truth and propaganda. It is, also, vital that all members of society, not just those who can afford the privilege, have the tools - the more complex language skills-to express themselves effectively.

For centuries, the English Language has been a vehicle for humane and democratic ideals, even being chosen in 1948, as the universal tongue in which to express the Human Rights Declaration. This generation must take care that it remains so.

Frances McKie's book, "Taking Command of the English Language", shows how this can be done by helping children to gain a firm grasp of the structure of their language so that they can go on to develop, in their reading, writing, talk and listening, keen analytic and mature expressive skills.

Anne Mackay MA (Hons) DipEd,
Retired Principal Teacher of English

INTRODUCTION

I have always felt quite certain that my own generation benefited from very clear, highly structured and progressive teaching of language throughout primary school. However, by the time I started to teach, the curriculum had changed. It became quite difficult to explain to older pupils why their own sentences were not making clear points or, sometimes, why the structure and sense had broken down completely.

To find out exactly where we stood at the beginning of secondary school, there was a very revealing test which challenged pupils to write three sentences. They were asked to use a word like "paint" or "dress" in the first sentence as a noun, in the next sentence as a verb and, thirdly, as an adjective. Most pupils, despite being able to chant vigorously that a noun was a "naming word", a verb was a "doing word" and an adjective was a "describing word", could not do this: they could certainly chant but they did not really understand the differences. At this important stage, half way through their school education, these problems were frustrating. It sometimes felt as if we were having to build on sand.

At the same time, we were also trying to help clever but perplexed senior students who could not understand why writing, "Othello smothered his wife with a pillow quaking with anger and suspicion," did not convey exactly what was meant. In response, I began to introduce lessons about the basic elements of language and the structure of sentences.

As a result, we began to have more effective conversations about the importance of word choice and word order in their own writing. Once pupils knew the rules, they became more enthusiastic about manipulating expression in all sorts of ways to improve clarity and impact. There also seemed to be overt satisfaction in the progressive nature of the lessons: their learning was tangible.

Perhaps, especially nowadays, in the age of texting, social media and emails, such concern with language structure might be dismissed as obsolete. It is, however, widely acknowledged that confident understanding of our own language is a vital step to success with other learning.

Knowing how to make ourselves understood, positively and effectively, in various situations, is empowering. Bombarded as we are, throughout the media, by so many forms of marketing and persuasion, it is also important to be able to recognise and understand the powerful effects of language techniques whenever we are watching, reading or listening. In these ways, such knowledge and understanding must surely lie at the heart of raising attainment and improving life chances for everyone.

Overall, therefore, this book is simply a compilation of lessons and materials that I developed as needs arose in classrooms: it is by no means a definitive account of current grammar rules. But I hope it will offer support to anyone who wants to become more confident about language skills and, especially, to all those who are keen to avoid dangerous, cycling post boxes!

SECTION 1:

WORK OF WORDS

This section looks at the work that words can do. Some words can do several different jobs, depending on where we find them.

THE WORK OF WORDS

We sort all our words into various groups, according to the work they are doing in a particular sentence.

Their three basic tasks are:
1. defining action: **verbs**
2. naming people, animals, places, objects and ideas: **nouns**
3. adding more details about nouns: **adjectives**

It is important to remember that the same word can do several different jobs.

Example

1. We can use the word *paint* as a **verb**:

I ***paint*** *the table white.*

2. We can use the word *paint* as a **noun**:

I used some ***paint*** *to cover the table.*

3. We can use the word *paint* as an **adjective**:

I bought this brush at the **paint** shop.

PRACTICE

In each of the following sentences you will find one of the following words:

dress toy play house shoe

Find the word and decide whether it has been used as a noun, a verb or an adjective.

1. We change into **play** clothes when we come home from school.
2. I lost a **shoe** on the beach.
3. They **dress** smartly on Sunday.
4. John tidied everything into the **toy** cupboard.
5. The children **play** happily in the park.
6. We have moved to a new **house**.
7. Mum cooked a huge pie for our **house** guests.
8. The blacksmith will **shoe** all the horses before he leaves.
9. You can buy new boots at the **shoe** shop.
10. She bought a blue **dress** for the party.
11. Cats often **toy** with the mice that they catch.
12. We enjoyed watching an exciting **play** at the theatre.
13. Dad built a big hutch and we **house** the rabbits in that.
14. They love to wander round the **dress** shops on Saturdays.
15. That ball is Jill's favourite **toy**.

SUMMARY

- Verbs, nouns and adjectives are the basic words of most sentences.
- It is very important to consider what work a word has done in a particular sentence before deciding that it is a verb, a noun or an adjective.

NOUNS

Nouns are words which act as **labels** for all the different things and people we talk about.

Example

The following sentences have all the nouns highlighted in bold type.

When **John** was cleaning the **house** he always started in the **kitchen**. He washed all the **dishes** and put them away in the **cupboard.** He scrubbed the **sinks,** all **surfaces** and the **floor**. The **bathroom** was next. After that, he hoovered the **corridors** and **stairs.** Once the **lounge** was tidied and cleaned, **John** usually sat down for a well-earned **rest**. He relaxed with a **coffee** and a massive chocolate **biscuit.**

PRACTICE

Play the **Shopping List** game!

In a group, take turns to add to your shopping list. Everyone must repeat the opening words: "Today I must remember to buy…" Then repeat all the items (nouns) already on the list, before adding one more.

MORE PRACTICE

Find all the nouns in the following passage.

In that street we saw a huge house surrounded by white walls. Three red cars sat outside. A green gate was open. Two ladies and a man quickly came out and jumped into the vehicles. They roared off towards the town and a dog started barking loudly in the garden.

Suddenly a policeman arrived on a motorbike. He spoke into his radio. Shortly afterwards a large van stopped at the kerb and more policemen leaped out.

Finally, we saw the police bring ten people, all wearing handcuffs, out of the building. We guessed they must be the criminals.

MORE ABOUT NOUNS

SINGULAR AND PLURAL

We say that a noun is **singular** when it refers to **only one** item.

We say that a noun is **plural** when it refers to **more than one** item.

Take care to follow the rules for making singular nouns into plural ones.

1.   Most nouns just add the letter **s** to change singular into plural.

one house	two house**s**
one dog	six dog**s**
one caravan	three caravan**s**

2.   Some nouns add **es**, especially if the singular noun already ends in **s**.

one loss	two loss**es**
one dress	five dress**es**

3.   If a noun ends in a vowel (a, e, i, o or u) before a **y**, we just add an **s**.

one donkey	four donkeys
one day	five days
one monkey	two monkeys

4. If a noun ends with a consonant before a **y**, we take away the **y** and add **ies**.

one fairy	three fair**ies**
one party	three part**ies**
one study	two stud**ies**

5. Some words do not change at all. The plural is the same as the singular.

one sheep	three sheep
one deer	six deer
one salmon	three salmon

6. As usual, in English, there are some interesting exceptions! In these cases there is a special word for the plural.

one child	four children
one person	seven people
one mouse	three mice
one ox	two oxen
one tooth	five teeth

PRACTICE

Turn the following singular nouns into plurals:

egg	month	story
diary	man	desk
bus	tooth	case
quay	dolly	mouse
lion	foot	house
goose	mummy	family
daddy	brother	lorry

USING THE APOSTROPHE

It is important, at this point, to say a few things about the **apostrophe**, the little comma that seems to float above words. This is because the apostrophe is often added incorrectly to the **s** in plural nouns.

- The apostrophe has *nothing* to do with making **plural nouns**.

- *Never* try to use an apostrophe to make a **singular noun** into a **plural noun**.

OWNERSHIP

The **only formal** job of the apostrophe is to show **ownership**.

Ownership and Singular Nouns

When we want to show that a singular noun owns something, we can add the apostrophe followed by the letter **s**.

Examples

the book *of the boy*: the boy**'s** book

the mane *of the horse*: the horse**'s** mane

the concern *of the father*: the father**'s** concern

NOTE

We use the apostrophe to show ownership when the owner is a living creature or human being. We do not usually use the apostrophe to show ownership when the owner is an object. In these cases we use the word: **of**.

Examples

The handle **of** the door.

The windows **of** the houses.

The points **of** the pencils.

NOTE

Even when a singular noun ends in **s**, we still add the apostrophe **and** the letter **s**.

This also applies to all proper names like James or Jess.

Example

The pencil of James: James**'s** pencil

Ownership and Plural Nouns

When a plural noun ends in **s** and we want to show that it owns something, we simply **add the apostrophe on its own**.

Examples

The books of the boys: the *boys'* books

The manes of the horses: the *horses'* manes

The concerns of the fathers: the *fathers'* concerns.

When a plural noun does **not** end in **s** we show ownership by adding an apostrophe followed by the letter **s**.

Examples

The toys of the children: the children's toys

The coats of the people: the people's coats

The hats of the men: the men's hats

NOTE

The apostrophe is **not** used to make the plural form of words like MP, CEO, TV, CD or DVD.

Just add the letter **s**.

Examples

Our neighbours have four TVs in their house.

Yesterday, the CEOs of all the major oil companies attended an important meeting in London.

The Apostrophe in Abbreviations (shortened words)

We should **not** shorten words when we are writing in **formal** English.

We **do** shorten words in **direct speech** and **informal writing**.

When we shorten words we use an apostrophe **to show where we have missed out letters**.

Examples

Formal: We **do not** buy theatre tickets very often because **they are** too expensive.

Informal: We **don't** buy theatre tickets very often because **they're** too expensive.

Formal: He **did not** come here because he **does not** want to join the club.

Informal: He **didn't** come here because he **doesn't** want to join the club.

Formal: We **could not, would not** and **should not** refuse to help.

Informal: We **couldn't, wouldn't** and **shouldn't** refuse to help.

NOTE

It's = it is

(We use the apostrophe to show that we have shortened **it is** by missing out the letter **i**.)

Example

We enjoy going to that beach because **it's** so near our village.

Its= of it

(We use **its** as an adjective in the same way we use **my, our, his** etc.)

Example

Edinburgh is a beautiful city but **its** popularity with tourists can make it seem crowded.

PRACTICE

Rewrite the following sentences and add apostrophes correctly when they are needed.

John entered the headmasters office. He gave his boss the lists of pupils who had taken part in the expedition and began to explain what had happened.

"All the teams were supposed to meet at the bridge and hike to the campsite together. Peters rucksack was too heavy and hed given some heavy water bottles to the others to carry for him. They hadnt minded at first but it wasnt long before they were all complaining. The younger boys voices were loudest because they were exhausted. Our leaders soon decided wed do better to set up the tents two miles from the campsite. Thats when things became really disastrous."

MORE ABOUT NOUNS

We also divide nouns into *common* and *proper* nouns.

Common nouns are names for a type of person, place or object. They do not have a capital letter.

Examples

city town desk pencil girl boy country

Proper nouns are special names given to just one person, place or object. They must always have a capital letter.

Examples

Carol Peter Latin Hampshire Plymouth

Special names often consist of several words. When this happens we give capital letters to the key words only.

Examples

House of Commons

United States of America

Marks and Spencer

Queen of the South

PRACTICE

Write out the following nouns.

Use a capital letter for proper nouns only.

edinburgh	central primary school
football	elephant
horse	european parliament
market	university
scotland	hampden football stadium
policeman	government
atlantic ocean	cooker
primary school	cupboard
house of commons	high street

MORE ABOUT NOUNS:

COLLECTIVE NOUNS

A collection is one, single group of the same sort of things, the same sort of people or the same sort of animals.

When we use a collective noun we treat it as a singular noun even though, inside the group, we have lots of people, animals or things.

Examples

One herd of cows **is grazing** in the field.

One flock of sheep **was running** across the hill.

One shoal of fish **was being chased** by a shark.

One group of boys **is playing football** in the park.

PRACTICE

Find out the **collective noun** for a group of each of the following:

books pupils geese wolves pigeons thieves footballers birds soldiers crows politicians musicians puppies ships tools singers drawers flowers stars stairs whales bees monkeys people lions arrows strawberries bananas

MORE PRACTICE

Choose 5 of these collective nouns and write a sentence for each one.

Remember to treat each collective noun as a **singular noun (*one collection*)**.

SUMMARY

- Common nouns are names which apply to ordinary examples of people, places or things.

- Common nouns are not given capital letters.

- Proper nouns are special names given to one particular person, place or thing.

- Proper nouns are given capital letters. Each key word of a special name is given a capital letter.

- Collective nouns are **always** treated as singular nouns.

- The apostrophe is **never** used to make a singular noun into a plural noun.

- The apostrophe is used to show ownership.

- The apostrophe can be used to shorten words in informal writing.

VERBS

THREE KEY POINTS ABOUT VERBS

1. Verbs tell us about the action in a sentence.
2. One verb may consist of several words.
3. Each verb can tell us several different things about the action.

Examples

The children **are racing** across the playground.

John **ate** his fish and chips very quickly.

We **had been wanting to buy** that car for a long time.

PERSONS of the VERB

FIRST PERSON

If we use a verb to show the action carried out by the **speaker** or **writer**, we say we are using the verb in the **First Person.**

Example

I am baking a cake. **I will eat** the cake for tea.

We were rushing to catch the bus. **We were** late for school.

SECOND PERSON

If we use a verb to show the action carried out by the **person** or **persons to whom we are speaking or writing**, we say we are using the verb in the **second person.**

Example

You have been waiting a long time. **You are** very patient.

THIRD PERSON

If we use a verb to show the action carried out by **the person or persons we are speaking or writing about,** we say we are using the verb in the **third person.**

Example

He was reading while **she spoke** quietly. **It was** a peaceful room. **They were working** hard.

SUMMARY

Verbs can be used in the **first person, second person** or **third person.**

Pronouns can show us which person is being used.

PERSON	SINGULAR	PLURAL
FIRST	I	we
SECOND	you	you
THIRD	he/she/it	they

PRACTICE

Find all the verbs in the following short passage. Decide whether they are in the first, second or third person:

I remember a time when we all went to the same little school on the island. One teacher taught all of us, together, in the same classroom. She organised us in groups according to how well we could read the same book.

Some of the bigger children felt quite angry about this. They teased the younger ones and they shouted rudely sometimes as we were going home after school.

I was walking beside wee Tam MacPherson one afternoon when a group of bigger boys started to jostle Tam.

"You are just a wee teacher's pet!" they yelled.

Tam ran off. He did not come back to school for a week.

TENSES OF THE VERB

Verbs tell us about action in the present, in the past and in the future.

There is a form of every verb for each time or **tense** and for each person, singular and plural.

In this way, for every time or tense, we have six options.

Example

PRESENT TENSE OF THE VERB:

TO WRITE

PERSON	SINGULAR	PLURAL
FIRST	I *write*	we *write*
SECOND	you *write*	you *write*
THIRD	he/she/it *writes*	they *write*

NOTE

There are two other ways of using the present tense.

1. I *am writing*; you *are writing*; he/she/it *is writing*; we *are writing*; you *are writing*; they *are writing*.

2. I *do write*; you *do write*; he/she/it *does write*; we *do write*; you *do write*; they *do write*.

25

Both these forms of the present tense show that *one* verb can consist of *two or more* words.

PAST PERFECT TENSE OF THE VERB:

TO WRITE

There are several ways of using the past tense. The simplest form is what we call the **Past Perfect Tense**. We use this form when the action has been **completed** in the past.

The first form of the Past Perfect Tense adds the **present tense of "to have"** to the **past participle** of the **main verb**.

PERSON	SINGULAR	PLURAL
FIRST	*I have* **written**	*we have* **written**
SECOND	*you have* **written**	*you have* **written**
THIRD	*he/she/it has* **written**	*they have* **written**

NOTE

There are two other ways of using the past perfect tense.

- I *wrote*; you *wrote*; he/she/it *wrote*; we *wrote*; you *wrote*; they *wrote*.

- I *did write*; you *did write*; he/she/it *did write*; we *did write*; you *did write*; they *did write*.

Some verbs make the **past perfect tense** and the **past participle** by simply adding -**ed.** They are called **regular verbs**.

Examples

I cook**ed**/ I have cook**ed**; I walk**ed**/ I have walk**ed**; I jump**ed**/ I have jump**ed**

However, many other verbs, like our example, **to write**, have different forms in the past tense. They are called **irregular verbs.**

Examples of Past Perfect Tenses

To go	I have gone	I went	I did go
To eat	I have eaten	I ate	I did eat
To teach	I have taught	I taught	I did teach
To swim	I have swum	I swam	I did swim
To drive	I have driven	I drove	I did drive
To sink	I have sunk	I sank	I did sink
To begin	I have begun	I began	I did begin
To sew	I have sewn	I sewed	I did sew
To be	I have been	I was	------------
To run	I have run	I ran	I did run

PAST IMPERFECT TENSE OF THE VERB:

TO WRITE

The Past Imperfect Tense is used to show that a main
verb in the past was **interrupted** or to show that we
do not know how long it lasted.

We make the Past Imperfect Tense by adding the
past tense of the **verb "to be"** to the **present
participle** of the **main verb**.

PERSON	SINGULAR	PLURAL
FIRST	*I was* **writing**	*we were* **writing**
SECOND	*you were* **writing**	*you were* **writing**
THIRD	*he/she/it was* **writing**	*they were* **writing**

NOTE

There is another way of using the past imperfect
tense.

I *used to write*; you *used to write*; he/she/it *used to write*;
we *used to write*; you *used to write*; they *used to write*.

Examples

The Smith family **used to live** in this street a long time ago.

The Smith family **were living** in this street until they moved to London.

I **used to fry** chips for every single meal.

I **was frying** some chips when the cooker exploded.

PRACTICE

Write five sentences which each use a verb in the Past Imperfect Tense.

PAST PLUPERFECT TENSE OF THE VERB:

TO WRITE

The Past Pluperfect Tense is used to show that one action happened **further back** in the past than another action.

It helps to show the order in which events occurred.

We make this tense by adding the **past tense** of the verb "to have" to the **past participle** of the **main verb**.

PERSON	SINGULAR	PLURAL
FIRST	*I had* **written**	*we had* **written**
SECOND	*you had* **written**	*you had* **written**
THIRD	*he/she/it had* **written**	*they had* **written**

Examples

I **had gone** to bed before the others arrived.

We ran all the way but the bus **had left** already.

PRACTICE

Write 5 sentences which use the Pluperfect Tense to show the order in which events happened in the past.

FUTURE TENSE OF THE VERB: TO WRITE

The Future Tense is made in the same way for all verbs.

We add the words **will** or **shall** to the main verb.

Person	Singular	Plural
First	I will/shall write	we shall/will write
Second	you will/shall write	you will/shall write
Third	he/she/it will/shall write	they will/shall write

MORE ABOUT VERBS

THE CONDITIONAL TENSE

As the name says, the **Conditional Tense** is used when we want to show something will happen only if a condition is met. It is not certain to happen.

The Conditional Tense is made by adding the words **could** or **would** to the main verb.

Examples

You **could be** a very fast runner if you train every day.

He **could have been injured** if the car had not stopped so quickly.

She **would like to come** to the party if she is invited.

We **would have offered to help** if you had asked us.

NOTE

A COMMON MISTAKE with the CONDITIONAL TENSE

Make sure you use the word **'have'** with this tense: do not confuse **'have'** with **'of'**. The word **'of'** is **never** used as a part of the Conditional Tense.

THE SUBJUNCTIVE MOOD

The Subjunctive is usually called a **mood** rather than a tense. It adds the words **may** or **might** to a verb. Like the conditional tense, it shows that something is not certain to happen. It is used to create a feeling of doubt. The subjunctive does not always add a condition.

Examples

The soldiers **may decide to attack** the castle or they **may march** past it.

You **might be allowed to go** to the party. On the other hand you **might be refused** permission.

They **might be trying to climb** through a window.

They **might try to break** the door.

MOODS of the VERB

When we refer to the **mood** of a verb, we are simply talking about **one** of **five ways** in which it can be used. As we have seen, we can use the **SUBJUNCTIVE**

MOOD to show doubt and uncertainty. There are **four** other **VERB MOODS.**

INFINITIVE MOOD

When we want to talk about a particular action, we can use the **infinitive mood** of the verb. The infinitive mood of every verb begins with the word **'to'.**

Examples

To lose my purse was a disaster; **to find** it under the table was a great relief.

To err is human; **to forgive** is divine.

INTERROGATIVE MOOD

When we ask a question, we are using the **interrogative mood** of the verb.

Examples

Are they hoping to stay with us tonight?

Will we be able to buy tickets for the match?

INDICATIVE MOOD

This is the straightforward form of every verb which we simply use **to indicate** action.

Examples

We drove our car to Glasgow.

The sheep have escaped from the field.

IMPERATIVE MOOD

The imperative mood is the form of the verb we use when we are giving other people instructions or orders. It is often used with an exclamation mark.

Examples

Send these parcels to Paris as quickly as possible!
Tell them to be quiet!

SUMMARY

- There are many different forms of every verb.

- Verbs can consist of several words.

- Using First, Second and Third Person shows who is telling the story.

- We can use verbs in either the Singular or Plural form.

- Tenses tell us about the time of events.

- The Conditional Tense shows something must happen before the next event can take place.

- The Subjunctive Mood creates doubt and uncertainty.

PRACTICE

Find all the verbs in the following passage. Make sure you spot all the words which make up each verb. Try to say as much as possible about the

Tense, Person, Number (Singular or Plural) in every case.

I still remember that wonderful holiday in the caravan. We had been hoping to hire a caravan for just four people but when we arrived the manager gave us a much bigger one for the same price. He also promised that if we paid a deposit we could use one of the rowing boats every day.

We were eating our breakfast on the first morning when someone knocked on the door. When David opened it he shouted in surprise. Our neighbours, John and Sally Brown, had also arrived the night before. They had spotted our car as they walked to the beach from their own caravan.

For the rest of the week we spent our time with them and their children. The weather was perfect and we enjoyed every minute.

Although we are much older now, we might go back there, this summer, just once more.

ADJECTIVES

Adjectives are the words we use to provide more information about nouns.

Examples

- We must catch the **big, red** bus to Glasgow for the **small, blue** bus goes to Edinburgh.

- We became **tired** and **hungry** during the **long, hot** journey to Glasgow.

- We carried our **heavy** suitcases to the **nearest** café and enjoyed an **excellent** snack of **tasty** sandwiches and **delicious, cool** smoothies.

- After that, we found out that the **best** way to get to our hotel was by taxi.

PRACTICE

Play the game called "The Minister's Cat".

In groups, following the alphabet, take turns to use an adjective to describe the minister's cat. At the end of the game the cat should have 26 adjectives!

We can use three grades of most adjectives.

1. The first grade is called the **positive** adjective.

2. The second grade is called the **comparative** adjective. We use this form when we are comparing two nouns.

3. The third grade is called the **superlative** adjective. We use this when we are comparing more than two nouns.

Examples

POSITIVE	COMPARATIVE	SUPERLATIVE
big	bigger	biggest
beautiful	more beautiful	most beautiful
few	fewer	fewest
many	more	most
good	better	best
bad	worse	worst

SUMMARY

- Many adjectives add **er** for the comparative form and **est** for the superlative form.

- Other adjectives add **more** for the comparative form and **most** for the superlative form.

- Some adjectives have their own special words for the comparative and the superlative form.

PRACTICE

Find the adjectives in the following sentences. Try to say whether they are in the positive, comparative or superlative form.

1. They have the most beautiful garden and donate many lovely flowers to charity events.
2. James was an excellent athlete but John was a better footballer.
3. Although the old man lived in a tiny, lonely cottage, he was the happiest person we knew.
4. Jane was the elder child and had left home to be married before her younger sister finished school.
5. When the gentle breeze suddenly became stronger we decided to return before worse weather arrived.

MORE ABOUT ADJECTIVES

Amount versus **Number**

When we write about the **quantity** of a noun we often use the adjectives: **many, more, much, most, few** and **little**. When we want to show the grades of these adjectives it is important to choose the right word.

To choose the right adjective, think about the difference between **mashed potato** and **chips**!

We **cannot count** mashed potato! We must refer to the **amount** or **size** of the portion on our plate. The adjectives for nouns that cannot be counted are little, less, least, much, more and most.

Example

Please give me less mashed potato with my meat.

We **can count** chips! The adjectives we use for nouns that **can be counted** are many, more, most, few, fewer and fewest.

Example

I would like fewer chips with my burger.

More Examples

I would love a few strawberries and a little cream please!

I would like many more flowers in the garden and much less mud!

ADVERBS

As the name makes clear, adverbs add information about verbs. They can tell us more about when (time), how (manner) and where (place) the action was completed. Many adverbs end in **–ly.**

ADVERBS OF TIME

often	tomorrow	after
seldom	firstly	next
now	always	

ADVERBS OF MANNER

kindly	carefully	quickly
slowly	gracefully	happily

ADVERBS OF PLACE

forwards	down	faraway
backwards	outside	nearby
everywhere	inside	here
up	there	somewhere

NOTE

Many adverbs can be graded in the same way as adjectives.

Examples

POSITIVE	COMPARATIVE	SUPERLATIVE
quickly	more quickly	most quickly
often	more often	most often
soon	sooner	soonest
fast	faster	fastest
angrily	more angrily	most angrily
carefully	more carefully	most carefully

PREPOSITIONS

Prepositions are little words, or groups of words, that usually tell us about position or direction in space or time. A preposition always creates a short phrase with the following noun. This phrase is called a Preposition Phrase.

Examples

The car *in front of* *that shop* belongs to Peter.

The horse jumped *over* *the fence.*

Jane arrived *before* *Ian.*

The dog *under* *the table* has stolen my food.

The spider sat *beside* *Miss Muffet.*

The children left *after* *the party.*

The letter is *from* London.

The shop *across* *the road* sells newspapers.

The soldiers marched *towards* *the castle.*

Peter ran *up* *the stairs.*

NOTE

If they appear on their own, some prepositions can also do the work of an **adverb**.

Examples

They came *across* to speak to us.

John fell *down*.

I have heard that *before*.

PRACTICE

Find all the preposition phrases in the following text.

They rushed across the platform to catch their train. John was carrying the heavy bags with both hands so Mary lifted the pram into the carriage. They soon found their seats but the train was very crowded so Mary kept Robert, their toddler, on her lap.

The conductor soon marched along the corridor to check their tickets. That was when Robert remembered he had left them at home, in his wallet, on the kitchen table.

Luckily Mary found the receipt inside her own purse. After a moment, the conductor accepted their explanation but still wrote their names and addresses in his little black book.

CONJUNCTIONS

Conjunctions are joining words. We can use conjunctions to join sentences together instead of separating them with full-stops. Conjunctions can also be used to join individual words and phrases together.

AND, BUT, OR and SO

Although they are small, these conjunctions are very powerful words, with special rules of their own. Use them carefully!

- These conjunctions are used only to join items that are equal or matching.

- They are called the **co-ordinating** conjunctions and tell us that the items on either side are equal, or that they are about the same topic.

- They can join a noun to a noun, a phrase to a phrase, a verb to a verb, a sentence to a sentence.

- They cannot join items which are not equal.

Examples

Apples, pears **and** oranges are popular fruits.

James, Peter **or** John can be the goalkeeper for the match.

The holiday was wonderful *but* expensive.

He forgot the time *so* he missed the bus.

There are many other conjunctions. Some of the most common include:

because	**when**
after	**though**
until	**unless**
as	**while**
since	**if**

PRACTICE

Read the following passage and find all the **co-ordinating** conjunctions. In each example, try to say as much as you can about the two items which are joined together.

Johnny and Peter set off up the mountain early in the morning. They were excited but nervous about the challenges ahead that day. They wanted to reach the top before midday so they travelled as quickly as possible. Their rucksacks were heavy with equipment including tents, ropes, extra clothing and food.

About two hours later the accident happened. Johnny had completed a steep part of the climb first and he was lowering a rope which would pull the heavy rucksacks up separately. The rope was caught on a sharp piece of rock. It was not possible to pull it up or down so Johnny climbed down to release it. He slipped and grabbed at the rock face but he became tangled in the rope. He was trapped and left hanging in the air.

Peter climbed up to help but he could not reach Johnny. Suddenly the rope broke away from the top and Johnny fell to the bottom, badly hurt.

Peter immediately phoned the emergency services for help. He explained that Johnny had injured both legs very badly so a helicopter was sent to rescue them.

SECTION 2:

SENTENCE

STRUCTURE

The most important unit of our language is the sentence. We usually define a sentence as a **group of words which makes complete sense on its own**.

English is a language that depends on structure and word order to make meaning clear. For all sentences, therefore, there are important rules which should be followed. When we do not follow the rules, the meaning can change so that our words no longer make clear sense.

There are two very important rules.

1. A sentence must have a complete verb.

2. A sentence must have a subject.

It is also important to use full-stops and other punctuation accurately so that sentences are clearly marked.

When sentences go wrong...

- Walking very unsteadily we saw the man climb into a car that had been drinking all night in the bar.

- John crashed into a post box cycling down the road and broke his nose which has been very sore for a long time and always looks where he is going now.

- In the summer I play tennis every Saturday at the local park. My friends wear white shorts which are very smart and always arrive before me.

- Still warm from the oven, Mum served cakes to the visitors that she had baked earlier that morning.

- The dog was caught by a policeman barking madly at a cat after he had stolen the sausages and quickly blew his whistle.

- With huge eyes and a beautiful, long brown tail, Mary adores her pony which is very gentle but always wears a hard hat to avoid accidents.

- A teacher was rushing into the classroom with a briefcase but boys were throwing rubbers and pencils at girls that were constantly flying through the air.

- At the college course, Susan and Jane met two very attractive boys who invited them out for dinner and rushed home to change into smart dresses.

When you have read the second section of this book,
you should be able to spot the problems
and sort out all these sentences
so that the meaning is clear!

A Few Reminders about Words

In order to work successfully with sentences, we need to be clear about the work each word in the sentence will do.

Words do three key jobs:

- We use them to show **what is happening (verbs)**.

- We use them as **names or labels (nouns)**.

- We use them to **explain more about nouns (adjectives)**.

Example

Look at these three sentences. Each sentence uses the word **paint** as a **verb** or a **noun** or an **adjective**. Try to say what work **paint** does in each sentence.

We went shopping to buy white **paint**.

We went to the **paint** shop to buy some new brushes,

They **paint** very beautiful pictures.

PRACTICE

Write three sentences using the word **dress** in the same ways: once as a verb, once as a noun and once as an adjective. Do the same with **cut** and **store**.

SUMMARY

- As you have seen, it is important to remember that one word can do several different jobs.

- It is always important to check what work each word is doing in a sentence.

BE CAREFUL WITH PRONOUNS!

Pronouns are helpful words which we often use to avoid having to repeat the same name several times in one sentence.

We organise them in three groups.

1. The first group is used when we are talking or writing about ourselves.

2. The second group is used for the people to whom we are talking or writing.

3. The third group is used when we are talking or writing about other people or things.

	SINGULAR	PLURAL
FIRST	I me mine	we us ours
SECOND	you yours	you yours
THIRD	he him his she her hers it	they them theirs

Example

The Smiths live next door to Andrew. Andrew loves working in the garden; the garden is beautiful. Jane often helps Andrew and Jane is an expert. Jane and Andrew work well together. Jane and Andrew recently grew some lovely tulips and gave some of the tulips to the Smiths.

We live next door to Andrew. **He** loves working in the garden; **it** is beautiful. Jane often helps **him** and **she** is an expert. **They** work well together. **They** recently grew lots of lovely tulips and gave some of **them** to **us**.

But be careful!
Make sure we know what the pronoun represents!

WHO DID WHAT?

The pronouns have become quite confusing! Decide what really happened in each of these short accounts. Then write them out more clearly.

Before the teacher entered the room, the boys and girls were fighting. They told them they would throw their pencils and rubbers at them. Then they ran out of the room and left them on their own. They were given a punishment exercise by the teacher. A girl stood crying in the corner. She said they had behaved very badly so it would be a large one. Then the others came back.

John met Mary in the park. Ben, her dog, was there and he gave her a box of chocolates. Ben was barking madly and running around. He was panting. He asked her if she would go out with him. Then Ben found a stinking old bone and started to dig a hole at her feet. Mary thanked him for the present and then dropped it in the hole by mistake. But worst of all he rolled in the mud and then jumped up and covered her in it.

It has been a busy night and they did not sleep very well. Mrs. Smith has been very sick. Mrs. Brown has a sore leg and the lady in the corner has a fever. It is important that she stays in her bed. Moving about too much has probably caused the sickness. She is having her leg examined by the doctor this morning. Make sure you give her the medicine in the cupboard. It is the one he gave her last night. That bed must be moved to the window. Remember to give her those new pills. They are next to it.

SUMMARY

- We must use pronouns very carefully to avoid confusion: they usually represent the noun (of same gender and number) immediately before them.

- Check the order of your points.

- Make sure your reader always knows what the pronoun represents!

SIMPLE SENTENCES

A sentence is a group of words that makes **clear sense** on its own.

Every sentence must have a **complete verb** and a **subject**.

A **simple** sentence tells us about **one event** only.

THE VERB (predicate) of a SENTENCE.

All sentences must contain a verb (also sometimes called the **predicate**). The verb is the part of the sentence that tells us about the **action** that has taken place.

For a sentence to work correctly the verb must be complete. It is important to remember that one verb often consists of several words, so we must find the whole verb in order to understand how the sentence works.

Example

John **threw** the ball.

John **had been throwing** the ball.

John **would have been throwing** the ball.

John **could have been trying to throw** the ball.

In each of these simple sentences, the verb is a form of **to throw**. In each case the verb contains a different number of words.

THE TROUBLE WITH PARTICIPLES

- Participles are words which have been made out of verbs.

- They sound like action words.

- On their own, they do the work of adjectives or nouns.

- Present Participles end in **-ing**.

- Past Participles often end in -**ed**.

- On their own, participles are **not** verbs.

- On their own, participles **cannot** make sentences.

PRESENT PARTICIPLE ADJECTIVES

We loved the **singing** star. (to sing)

She joined the **dancing** team. (to dance)

He drove the **racing** car. (to race)

PRESENT PARTICIPLE NOUNS

I enjoyed **the swimming**. (to swim)

I loved **the cheering**. (to cheer)

I stopped **the fighting**. (to fight)

PAST PARTICIPLE ADJECTIVES

I saw the **broken** window. (to break)

He ate the **boiled** potatoes. (to boil)

They bought the **painted** house. (to paint)

PARTICIPLES AS PARTS OF VERBS

A participle is often **part** of a verb which consists of several words.

Examples
I **have been** *running*.
She **had** *eaten*.
He **will have been** *coming*.
The stew **had been** *cooked*.
They **have** *gone*.

PRACTICE
Look at the following pairs of sentences. From each pair, work out which one is a complete sentence and which one is not. Try to explain why.

1. The snow was falling heavily in the wood.
   The snow falling through the dark trees and the dog barking.
2. Children having sung several beautiful songs.
   The children had sung several beautiful songs.
3. The room tidy and the lights having been switched off.

59

Having tidied the room we switched off the lights.

4. We were driving fast along the motorway on a very warm day.

   A very warm day and driving fast along the motorway.

5. Annoyed by the flies, the poor horse had been swishing his tail to keep them away.

   The horse annoyed by flies in the heat and swishing his tail to keep them away.

SUMMARY

- Be careful with participles!
- Participles look like action words but are **not verbs** on their own.
- A participle, on its own, **cannot be the verb** for a sentence.

Commands (Imperatives)

The shortest sentences are often commands. They usually end with an exclamation mark.

The word **you** is understood to begin every command, even if it does not actually appear in the sentence.

Come here at once! Stop doing that!

Some commands can consist of only one word.

Stop! Stand! Sit! March! Attack!

THE SUBJECT OF A SENTENCE

We have shown that, to become a sentence, a group of words must, first of all, have a complete **VERB**.

The other vital part of a sentence is the **SUBJECT**.

The **SUBJECT** is the part which does the action.

We can always find the subject by asking this question:

Who or what + the verb ?

The answer is the **SUBJECT** of that sentence.

Example

The policeman had arrested the thief.

VERB: had arrested

QUESTION: Who or what had arrested?

SUBJECT: The policeman

PRACTICE

Find the verb and the subject in each of the following simple sentences.

Find the **verb** first.

In order to find the **subject**, ask the question: Who or what + verb?

1. The horses had been galloping.
2. Peter was sleeping.
3. The ships will be sailing.
4. Jane would have liked to sing.
5. I have arrived.

MORE PRACTICE

- Make up five sentences of your own.
- Mark the verb and the subject in each one.

THE OBJECT OF A SENTENCE

All sentences must have a **VERB** and a **SUBJECT**.

The **VERB** is the action part of the sentence.

The **SUBJECT** tells us who or what did the action.

Sentences often, but not always, also contain an **OBJECT**.

The **OBJECT** of the sentence tells us who or what had the action done to them.

Example

John was throwing the ball.

VERB: was throwing

SUBJECT: John

OBJECT: the ball

To find the object of any sentence, ask the following question:

SUBJECT + VERB + whom or what?

The answer will be the **OBJECT**.

QUESTION: John was throwing whom or what?

OBJECT: the ball

ACTIVE and PASSIVE VERBS

In sentences where there is a **DIRECT OBJECT**, we can make the verb **ACTIVE** or **PASSIVE**.

- The verb is **active** when the subject of the sentence is responsible for the action.
- The verb is **passive** when the subject of the sentence is **not** responsible for the action.
- **Passive** verbs are often accompanied by **a phrase** beginning with '**by**'.

Examples
ACTIVE   John **shut** the door.
PASSIVE The door **was shut** *by* John.

ACTIVE   The farmer **will have ploughed** that field before nightfall.
PASSIVE That field **will have been ploughed** *by* the farmer before nightfall.

NOTE
If we use a **PASSIVE VERB**, we can still find the **Subject** and **Verb** by asking our questions.
There will **no longer** be an **object**.

Example
VERB: was shut

Find the SUBJECT: WHO or WHAT **was shut?**
SUBJECT= the door

"by John" is now a **phrase** telling us **how** the action was completed.

PRACTICE

Find the **VERB**, then the **SUBJECT** and then the **OBJECT** in the following sentences.

Remember that the verb, the subject and the object of a sentence can each consist of **several** words.

1. The girls had been playing tennis.
2. Peter loves to eat sausage and chips.
3. We would like to see your holiday photographs.
4. Those children have eaten too much chocolate.
5. You might have tried to clean that awful mess!
6. The storm has wrecked all the tents.

MORE PRACTICE

Not all sentences contain an object. In the following sentences, use the questions to check verb and subject. Then decide whether or not the sentence contains an object.

1. The whole class has visited the museum.
2. They ought to have come.
3. I would love to watch that film.
4. They are resting.
5. He must have been running!

6. They have collected all the rubbish.
7. The crowd rushed along the road.
8. Many people have climbed that mountain.
9. The bus is running late today.
10. John will return to France in December.

INDIRECT OBJECT

A simple sentence tells us about a single event.

- It must contain a **VERB** and a **SUBJECT**.

- It will often include an **OBJECT**.

- It can also tell us about an **INDIRECT OBJECT**.

The best way to think about this is to remember that the **OBJECT** had the action **directly done** to it.

The **INDIRECT OBJECT** has **not** had something directly done to it, but is still **indirectly** affected by the event in some way.

Example

Peter tidied the room for his mother.

VERB: tidied

SUBJECT: Peter

OBJECT: room

*His mother was **indirectly affected** by his action. She did not have to tidy the room herself.*

INDIRECT OBJECT: his mother

Example

Jane bought her brother a new football.

VERB: bought

SUBJECT: Jane

OBJECT: football

Her brother was **indirectly affected** *by Jane's action. He ended up with a new football.*

NOTE

The indirect object is usually found **just before the object** or after the words *to* or *for.*

PRACTICE

Find the **verb, subject, object and indirect object** in the following sentences.

1. He has given me a beautiful bunch of flowers.
2. Jane had baked a delicious cake for her friend.
3. I used to send her a birthday card.
4. They must buy Peter some new boots for winter weather.
5. His father bought him that amazing car.
6. John will have to post that parcel for Dad.
7. I explained the situation to him.
8. The policeman gave that driver a warning.

PRACTICE

Add the indirect object to the following sentences.

Place the indirect object **immediately in front** of the object or use the words **to** or **for.**

1. On his birthday, we brought his favourite doughnuts. (John)

2. The school provided smart football jerseys. (the team)

3. After the storm neighbours repaired the fence. (the old couple)

4. Mr Smith sent an angry letter about litter. (the council)

5. They built a flat above the garage. (their elderly parents)

6. The rich landowner gave a whole field. (the village)

7. Their mum loves to read a story every night at bedtime. (the twins)

8. At the start of the lesson the teacher showed the new formula. (us)

QUESTION STRUCTURE

To turn a simple sentence into a question, we change the order of words. This can mean that the subject appears in the middle of the verb.

Example
They have broken the window.
VERB: have broken
SUBJECT: They
OBJECT: the window

QUESTION
Have they **broken** the window?

PRACTICE
Find the **VERB, SUBJECT** and **OBJECT** in the following questions.

1. Did they enjoy the party?
2. Have you finished your homework?
3. Would you like to buy this house?
4. Has John forgotten his coat?
5. Should I have locked the door?

SUMMARY

- All sentences must contain a complete verb.

- A simple sentence tells us about a single event.

- The verb is the action part of a sentence.

- The verb in a sentence can consist of several words.

- All sentences must contain a subject.

- The subject does the action.

- Sentences can also contain an object.

- The object has the action done to it.

- An indirect object does **not** have the action done to it but *is indirectly affected* by the same event.

- An indirect object will appear immediately in front of the object or after the words **to** or **for**.

- A sentence can be turned into a question by changing the order of the words.

PHRASES

To add information to simple sentences we can use small groups of words as well as individual adjectives and adverbs. These groups are called **phrases**. They do not contain an SV group (Subject+ Verb) so they cannot stand on their own. They are always added to provide extra information.

Adjective phrases: as small as an ant; kinder than the others; full of joy; perfectly neat

Preposition phrases: over the wall; before the party; in the box; in front of the door

Adverb phrases: as fast as possible; as quietly as a mouse

Participle phrases: jumping with joy; shaking with fear; hopping over the table

Example

Shouting encouragement from the terraces, they supported their football team at the city stadium.

NOTE

Phrases which give more information about the subject or object of a sentence will always describe the noun or pronoun nearest to them.

Phrases can never stand on their own. They must always be part of a complete sentence which already contains an SV group.

PRACTICE

Find the verb, subject and the phrases in the following sentences.

1. Rounding them up, the clever collie dog guided the sheep over the hill and into the shed.

2. After the meeting the crowd marched with great excitement along the road.

3. In the very hot sun, John still looked as cool as a cucumber.

4. Kicking the ball over the goalkeeper's head Peter scored an amazing goal.

5. Packed with holiday clothes, their suitcases sat in a row beside the front door.

SUMMARY

- Phrases are small groups of words which do not contain an SV group.

- Phrases are used to add information to subjects, verbs or objects within a sentence.

- Adjective phrases will always describe the noun or pronoun nearest to them.

- Phrases must never be given a capital letter and full-stop on their own.
- A phrase can only be part of a complete sentence.

EXTENDING THE SIMPLE SENTENCE

A simple sentence contains only one event. It must have a verb and a subject (an **SV group**) and sometimes it has an object and an indirect object.

Example

John gave his wife a present.

We can extend this simple sentence by adding more information about each part.

We can use adjectives and phrases to describe the subject and the object.

We can use adverbs and phrases to add information about the verb. The extensions of the verb will tell us more about **when, where, how** or **why** the action took place.

Example

Shaking with excitement, John quickly gave his surprised wife a huge present.

NOTE

- Adjective phrases and adjectives will **always** describe the noun nearest to them.

- Be careful not to break this rule. Your meaning may be lost.

Example

John quickly gave his surprised wife a huge present, shaking with excitement.

Presents do not, normally, shake with excitement!

PRACTICE

In the following sentences find the verb, subject and object.

Extend the verb with words and phrases to answer these questions:

How? When? Where? and Why?

1. They planned their holiday.
2. Peter won the race.
3. The storm destroyed the wood.
4. Mary baked a cake.
5. The policeman caught the robber.

MORE PRACTICE

In the following sentences find the verb, subject and object.

Say which words and phrases extend the subject, verb or object.

1. Early that morning, the hard-working servants had cleaned the old, rambling house very thoroughly.

2. Rushing down the street, the old lady suddenly dropped her huge bag.

3. Yesterday my poor old dad accidentally crashed his brand new car into the tree outside our house.

4. Throughout the summer huge bees have been appearing in our garden.

5. Tired and hungry, John finally reached the remote campsite just before dark.

MORE PRACTICE

In the following sentences find the verb, subject and, if they are there, the object and indirect object.

Add adjectives and phrases to the subject and object.

Add adverbs and phrases to the verb to give more information about **when, why, how** or **where** the action took place.

NOTE

Be careful not to add another SV group. Simple sentences contain one SV group only.

1. The ship left the harbour.
2. James scored the goal.
3. The couple decided to buy the house.
4. Her neighbour brought the lady food.

5. The family enjoy a holiday.
6. The burglar entered the house.
7. The survivor told the reporters his story.
8. The waves struck the pier.

SUMMARY

- Extending the subject, verb and object of a simple sentence adds useful information.
- We extend the subject and the object with adjectives and phrases.
- These adjectives and phrases will describe the noun or pronoun nearest to them.
- It is vital to place the extensions in the correct place to make complete sense.
- Verbs are extended with adverbs and phrases.
- Extensions to verbs tell us more about **when, why, how** or **where** the action took place.
- Extensions must never contain another subject and verb (SV) group. This is because a simple sentence must have only one SV group.

PUNCTUATION OF SENTENCES

A sentence must be **separated** from other sentences or **joined** to them.

Punctuation marks are used to **separate** sentences.

Punctuation marks which can be used to **separate** sentences are:

1. Full-stops
2. Colons
3. Semi-colons
4. Exclamation marks
5. Question marks

Full-stops are the usual way to separate sentences. A full-stop must be followed by a capital letter, beginning the next sentence.

Example

He stopped the car. She jumped out.

Colons can be used to separate sentences in order to show that the second sentence is an illustration or explanation of the point made in the first one. The second sentence does **not** begin with a capital letter.

Example

John loves travelling: he visits several new countries every year.

NOTE

A dash can be used in exactly the same way as a colon.

Semi-colons can be used to separate sentences to show that the next sentence is on the same subject as the previous one.

Example

Oranges are not normally grown in the UK; lemons and bananas are also imported from other countries.

Exclamation Marks are used to indicate a command or strong feelings.

Example

Stop right there! He was furious!

Question Marks simply indicate that a question is being asked.

PRACTICE

Find the SV groups in the following sentences.

Punctuate them using the most suitable punctuation marks.

1. Jane works very hard she also plays lots of sports

2. Edinburgh is a very beautiful city elegant buildings line many streets the castle stands high on a huge rock

3. John will not be coming to the party he must finish his homework

4. Are you really going to eat all those cakes put them back immediately

5. The storm broke rain pelted the streets trees bent right over in the wind rubbish flew high in the air

6. Mary apologised for missing the meeting she had been stuck in a traffic jam

7. We are very fond of fruit pies for dessert we also love ice cream

8. There were many beautiful trees in the wood rowan beech and birch all glowed in the autumn light

---

SUMMARY

- Sentences can be separated from each other with the correct use of punctuation marks.

- Punctuation marks which can be used to separate sentences are:

Full-stops, Colon (or Dash), Semi-colon, Question Mark, Exclamation Mark.

A VERY IMPORTANT NOTE ABOUT COMMAS

A comma can **never** be used to separate sentences. Commas are used mainly:

- to separate items in a list
- before opening direct speech
- to indicate parenthesis (see below)

Using a comma incorrectly to separate sentences can accidentally change the meaning of what you have written.

Example

John was certain he would fail, however he tried.

John was certain he would fail. However he tried.

Parenthesis

This is just a method of using punctuation to show that the writer has added extra information to the basic point. It can be removed without destroying the sense. The extra information will be set between two **commas** or two **dashes** or two **brackets.**

Examples

John, a clever man, earns a lot of money.

They saw the car- a red saloon- speeding down the road.

London (the capital city of England) is one of the largest cities in the world.

NOTE

There is more information about parenthesis in Section 3.

SUMMARY

Commas are used:

- to separate items in a list

- before opening direct speech

- to indicate parenthesis

Commas **cannot be used** to separate sentences.

COMPOUND AND COMPLEX SENTENCES

Compound and complex sentences are sentences which have more than one SV group. They have been created by **joining** two or more simple sentences together.

CLAUSES

As soon as we **join** sentences together, so that they become parts of a bigger sentence, we call them **clauses**.

In a complex sentence, we call one clause **the main event**. We use the other clauses to give us more information about **the main event**.

Making a Complex Sentence

The bell rang. **The children yelled.** (2 sentences)

When the bell rang **the children yelled.** (complex sentence with 2 clauses)

- The clause with the **main event (the children yelled)** is called the **principal clause.** It stays exactly the same.

- This **principal clause**, unaltered, can still stand on its own as a sentence and can still be given a capital letter and full-stop.

- We call the other **altered, less important** clauses the **subordinate clauses**.

- **Subordinate clauses can no longer stand on their own** and, for that reason, cannot be given a full-stop and capital letter.

- The simplest way to turn a sentence into a subordinate clause is to add a **subordinating conjunction**.

- Some **subordinating conjunctions** include:

  when, while, although, because, since, after, before, until, unless, so that, as

Example

Ian made the tea.

Joan laid the table.

Both of these simple sentences make complete sense and each can stand alone.

MAKING THEM INTO A COMPLEX SENTENCE

- *Ian made the tea*

  stays the same and becomes the **principal clause**.

- **while** *Joan laid the table*

  "while" has been added to make this sentence the **subordinate clause**.

  It now tells us **when** the **main event** took place.

85

NEW COMPLEX SENTENCE

While Joan laid the table Ian made the tea.

Another Example

The weather was very cold.

They cancelled the football match.

MAKING THEM INTO A COMPLEX SENTENCE

- *They cancelled the football match*

  stays the same and becomes the **principal clause**.

- ***because*** *the weather was very cold*

  "because" has been added to make this sentence the **subordinate clause**.

  It tells us **why** the **main event** took place.

NEW COMPLEX SENTENCE

Because the weather was very cold they cancelled the football match.

NOTE

This complex sentence begins with a subordinate clause. As long as the subordinate clause is added to a principal clause, the complex sentence is correct.

PRACTICE

Turn the following pairs of sentences into complex sentences, using the given subordinate conjunction.

1. You shouted at me. I still love you. **although**

2. He has arrived late. He has missed lunch. **because**

3. John leaves school next year. He will work hard. **until**

4. Mary moved house. She has been very happy. **since**

5. They enjoyed a large supper. They went to bed. **after**

6. You have worked so well. You can go home now. **as**

7. We are going to be very late. The train speeds up. **unless**

8. We drove off to London that morning. Mary fell down the stairs. **before**

MORE PRACTICE

Find the **principal clause**, the **subordinate clause** and the **subordinating conjunction** in each of the following **complex sentences**.

1. I will not go unless you come with me.

2. Jane screamed when the window opened.

3. Although I work hard I do not earn much money.

4. Because the wood was so damp we could not light a fire.

5. While the Browns were on holiday in Spain they met their neighbours in the same resort.

6. I was reading a book quietly before they arrived.

7. Mary led the walking group since she knew the area very well.

8. Mum always listens to the radio while she drives to work.

9. I will not come until you invite me.

10. After the visitor left we discovered her handbag under a chair.

THREE TROUBLESOME WORDS

Simple Sentences must be separated by a punctuation mark or joined together with conjunctions.

The following three troublesome words often cause confusion because they cannot be used to join sentences together.

HOWEVER   THEREFORE   THEN

These words cause a lot of mistakes in sentences.

All three words are **adverbs**, words which add information to a verb.

They are **not** conjunctions. They cannot be used to join sentences together.

When they are used incorrectly they can destroy the meaning of a sentence.

Make sure you always use them **only** as **adverbs**.

PRACTICE

Read the following sentences.

a)   It was a very small town then. The new factory brought many more people to live there.

b) It was a very small town. Then the new factory brought many more people to live there.

*The meaning changes when **then** is moved from one sentence to the other.*

Read the sentences again, this time joined together with the conjunction 'but'.

a) It was a very small town **then but** the new factory brought many more people to live there.

b) It was a very small town **but then** the new factory brought many more people to live there.

*The meaning still changes when **then** is moved from one sentence to another.*

Read this sentence in which someone has made the mistake of trying to use 'then' as a conjunction.

It was a very small town then the new factory brought many more people to live there.

In this sentence there is no punctuation separating the two simple sentences and there is no conjunction showing us where the join has been made. We do not know whether "then" belongs to the first sentence or the second sentence. The meaning is not clear.

HOWEVER and THEREFORE

a) Romeo made many mistakes **however**. Juliet loved him, all the same.

b) Romeo made many mistakes. **However** Juliet loved him, all the same.

c) Romeo made many mistakes **however** Juliet loved him all the same.

In the first two sentences the meaning changes when "however" moves from one sentence to another.

In the third sentence there is no punctuation separating the two simple sentences and there is no conjunction showing us where the join has been made. We do not know whether the adverb "however" belongs to the first sentence or the second sentence. The meaning is not clear.

a) They have no choice therefore. They must leave the country.

b) They have no choice. **Therefore** they must leave the country.

c) They have no choice **therefore** they must leave the country.

In the first two sentences the meaning changes when "therefore" moves from one sentence to another.

In the third sentence there is no punctuation separating the two simple sentences and there is no conjunction showing us where the join has been made. We do not know whether the adverb "therefore" belongs to the first sentence or the second sentence. The meaning is not clear.

SUMMARY

- We can join simple sentences together to make complex sentences.

- When a sentence becomes part of a complex sentence it is called a clause.

- A complex sentence keeps one simple sentence, about the main event, exactly as it was.

- This is called the principal clause.

- We can add subordinating conjunctions to the other sentences.

- They become the subordinate clauses.

- Subordinate clauses tell us more about the principal clause.

- Subordinate clauses cannot stand on their own. They must be attached to a principal clause in a longer sentence.

- We can start a complex sentence with a subordinate clause, as long as it is linked to a principal clause.

- We cannot use **however**, **therefore** or **then** as conjunctions to join sentences. They are adverbs.

NOTE

We have just looked at the trouble which can arise if we try to use **however, then** or **therefore** as conjunctions to join sentences together.

There is another **very** common mistake. It usually happens when we have tried to use one of these words, incorrectly, as a conjunction and then try to add **a comma** to mark the end of the sentence.

Example
We wanted to say this:

Dad always made a dreadful mess in the kitchen. He tried, however, to cook breakfast.

Comma Splice

Dad always made a dreadful mess in the kitchen, however he tried to cook breakfast.

Comma Splice

Dad always made a dreadful mess in the kitchen however, he tried to cook breakfast.

Commas **cannot** be used as full-stops. Trying to use a comma between two sentences is a **serious mistake** which is known as a **comma splice**.

SUMMARY

Separate sentences with correct punctuation.

- Join sentences with correct use of conjunctions.
- Never try to **join** sentences with **however, then** or **therefore**.
- Never try to **separate** sentences with a **comma**.

SUBORDINATE RELATIVE CLAUSES

A special situation arises when we want to join together two sentences which share a common feature.

We can now use one of **five relative pronouns** as a **joining word.**

WHO   WHOM   WHICH   THAT   WHOSE

Key Points

- When we join the sentences together in a complex sentence, we leave one sentence exactly as it was.

- It describes **the main event** and is now called the **principal clause**.

- We **remove** the common feature from the other sentence and **replace** it with a **relative pronoun**.

- This sentence is now called a **subordinate relative clause**.

- Subordinate relative clauses have one extra rule which is very important:

- In the new complex sentence the subordinate relative clause **must be inserted immediately after the common feature**.

Examples

The man had dark hair.

The man stole a car.

The common feature is **the man**.

First sentence becomes a subordinate clause: **who** had dark hair.

New Complex Sentence

The man **WHO had dark hair** stole a car.

- *If we use the wrong order this becomes: the man stole a car who had dark hair.*

The lady bought **a red coat**.

The red coat had a hood.

The common feature is **red coat**.

Second sentence becomes a subordinate clause: **which** had a hood.

New Complex Sentence

The lady bought a red coat **WHICH had a hood.**

- *If we use the wrong order this becomes: the lady which had a hood bought a red coat.*

The house was burgled.

The house had a green roof.

The common feature is **house**.

Second sentence becomes a subordinate clause: **that** was burgled.

New Complex Sentence

The house **THAT** was burgled had a green roof.

* *If we use the wrong order this becomes: the house had a green roof that was burgled.*

The boy had two dogs.

The boy's mother was a vet.

The common feature is **boy**.

Second sentence becomes a subordinate clause: **whose** mother was a vet.

New Complex Sentence

The boy **WHOSE mother was a vet** had two dogs.

* *If we use the wrong order this becomes: the boy had two dogs whose mother was a vet.*

SPECIAL NOTE: WHOM

Whom is used to replace a common feature which is the **object** of the subordinate relative clause. It is not used very much nowadays. However, it is important to remember that it is also placed at the **beginning** of the subordinate clause.

Example

Peter just annoyed that person very badly.

That person is his new boss.

The first sentence becomes a subordinate clause: **whom** Peter just annoyed very badly.

New Complex Sentence

That person **whom** Peter just annoyed very badly is his new boss.

PRACTICE
WHO WHOM WHICH WHOSE THAT

Use one of these relative pronouns to join each of the following pairs of sentences together in a complex sentence.

1. The house was very large.
    They bought the house.
2. The boy was angry.
    I lost the boy's ball.
3. The sweets are delicious.
    The sweets are in the dish.
4. The lady won the lottery.
    The lady is my neighbour.
5. Jane and Peter are going to be married.
    I know Jane and Peter very well.
6. John's father plays football for Scotland.
    John is a pupil at our school.
7. I hope to finish the marathon.
    The marathon is a huge challenge.

8. People take regular exercise.
   People are thought to be healthier.
9. Mary read the book.
   The book was recommended by her teacher.
10. We booked the hotel.
    The hotel was given five stars by the tourist board.

SUMMARY

- When two sentences share a common feature they can be joined together by one of the five relative pronouns.

- The five relative pronouns are:

  which who whom whose that

- One sentence stays exactly the same. It is the principal clause. It can stand on its own.

- The other sentence replaces the common feature with a relative pronoun.

- It is now a subordinate relative clause. It can no longer stand on its own.

- The relative pronoun is usually the first word of a subordinate clause.

- The subordinate clause must always be placed immediately after the common feature in the new complex sentence.

MORE PRACTICE

- The following complex sentences each contain a principal clause and various subordinate clauses, including subordinate relative clauses.

- Identify each Subject/Verb group.

- Find the principal clause and then the subordinate clauses which add information to it.

- Write down the subordinating conjunctions and the relative pronouns which begin each subordinate clause.

1. When we reached the station John, who was carrying the heaviest bags, gave a huge sigh of relief.

2. He intends to visit the shopkeeper who sold us the computer because it has never worked properly.

3. Jean, who loves her garden, buys her plants from these suppliers as they have a good reputation.

4. Since he returned to school, Peter has had to work very hard because he has missed so much classwork.

5. The first disaster happened when they forgot the rucksack that contained all the food.

6. After we left the train we visited the old station café which had been modernised.

7. Because it started to rain, I opened my umbrella which was immediately ripped by the strong wind.

8. Although they were extremely excited while they performed on the stage, the small children, whose

parents sat in the audience, behaved like professionals.

SUBORDINATE NOUN CLAUSE

This subordinate clause has a very interesting job because it gives us the story behind the **subject** or the **object** in a sentence. This is why we call it a **noun** clause.

Examples

John announced *the news.* In this sentence the **object** is the **noun:** *news.*

John announced *that he was leaving his job.*

In this sentence the **object** is the **noun clause:** *that he was leaving his job.*

Mary's skill is widely known. In this sentence the **subject** is the **noun:** *skill.*

That Mary makes excellent chocolate cakes is widely known.

In this sentence the **subject** is the **noun clause:** *that Mary makes excellent chocolate cakes.*

They wanted to know the plan. In this sentence the **object** is the **noun:** *plan.*

They wanted to know *what they should do next.*

In this sentence the **object** is the **noun clause:** *what they should do next.*

COMPOUND

SENTENCES

A compound sentence is a sentence which contains two or more principal clauses. This happens when we join two simple sentences together with special conjunctions that do **not** make one event more important than the other.

AND   BUT   OR   SO

Remember! Although these are very small words, they are also **very powerful**. They insist that the two items they are joining are of equal value. It is very important to use them correctly.

Examples

- Ian had a dog. Peter had a cat.

  Compound Sentence (with 2 principal clauses):

  Ian had a dog **but** Peter had a cat.

- Ian had a dog. The dog hated cats. Peter had a cat.

  Compound Sentence (with 2 principal clauses and 1 subordinate clause):

  Ian had a dog **which** hated cats **and** Peter had a cat.

- Ian had a dog. The dog hated cats. Peter had a cat. Peter did not like dogs.

  Compound Sentence (with 2 principal clauses and 2 subordinate clauses):

  Ian had a dog which hated cats but Peter had a cat because he did not like dogs.

- They went on holiday. Peter carefully planned the route. The route took them through the Lake District. Ian booked the hotel. He knew the owner.

  Compound Sentence (with 2 principal clauses, 1 subordinate relative clause and two other subordinate clauses):

  Before they went on holiday, Peter carefully planned the route which took them through the Lake District and Ian booked the hotel because he knew the owner.

AND   BUT   OR   SO

As you have seen, these joining words are special because, although they are small words, they carry a **very powerful message.** They signal that the two things they are joining **have the same value**.

This can mean they are joining two nouns, two adjectives, two verbs, two phrases or two sentences or two clauses.

They will **not** join two things which are not equal.

For this reason, they are called **co-ordinating** (matching) conjunctions.

They can cause a lot of trouble if we do not use them correctly. If we did not mean the words on either side of these conjunctions **to be treated as equals, doing the same job,** the reader will be misled.

Look at this example from page 46:

My friends wear white shorts which are very smart **and** always arrive before me.

The original three sentences were:

1. My friends wear white shorts.
2. The shorts are very smart.
3. My friends always arrive before me.

THE CORRECTIONS

Using "and" to join two of the original sentences together would work *if we joined the* **two that refer to the friends**:

My friends always arrive before me **and** wear white shorts which are very smart.

The co-ordinating conjunction 'and' tells us that the clauses on either side of it are both about the **friends**.

SUMMARY

- Co-ordinating conjunctions must be used very carefully.

- They signal that the words on either side of them are of equal value or about the same subject.

- Make sure you place them correctly, especially in longer sentences.

PRACTICE

Turn the following groups of sentences into compound sentences, using the conjunctions and relative pronouns that have been given.

1. but / who

James is a very clever boy.

James hopes to become a vet.

Jane is very athletic.

Jane wants to be a gymnast.

2. which / but / because

They had slept in.

They ran all the way.

The bus had already gone.

They had been hoping to catch the bus.

3. which / as / and

Do not be late for tea.

Your friends will be here.

The chips will be spoiled.

You love to eat chips.

4. **because / who / when / and**

The swimming lesson started.

Jane refused to enter the water.

She was terrified of drowning.

Peter stupidly pushed her into the pool.

He wanted to have fun.

5. which / since / but

They were going on holiday.

They cancelled the papers.

They forgot to cancel the milk.

The milk piled up on their doorstep.

MORE PRACTICE

Read the following compound sentences and find:

- principal clauses
- subordinate clauses
- subordinate relative clauses
- relative pronouns
- conjunctions

1. After Peter leaves school he could go to college or he might decide to work on his father's farm.

2. Mary turned on the oven before she started baking but it was still cold when the cakes were ready to cook.

3. The bus was very late because the weather was stormy so James ordered a taxi which arrived very quickly.

4. Because it is a cheap form of holiday we used to go camping every summer but now we can afford to stay in hotels and I am very happy about that.

5. After he had cleaned the bathroom, John started to hoover the stairs but he was interrupted by the phone call which he had been expecting.

6. Because she was feeling poorly old Mrs Grant walked slowly so she missed the bus which would have taken her to the hospital.

7. Unless we have much more rain soon there will be a very poor harvest and local farmers who depend on these crops will lose a great deal of money.

8. Before they were married they lived in Edinburgh but they have now moved to London which is a much bigger city.

SUMMARY

- Compound sentences have two or more principal clauses.

- This means that at least two simple sentences have not been altered. They are equally important within the compound sentence.

- Coordinating conjunctions (and, but, so, or) always join items that are the same or equal. They can also signal that the two clauses on either side are about the same subject.

- Compound sentences can also contain subordinate relative clauses and subordinate clauses to give extra information about the main events.

- In compound sentences it is especially important to make sure the clauses are placed accurately so that the meaning is clear.

REVISION

SIMPLE SENTENCES

*(Remember: simple sentences have just **one** verb and **one** subject.)*

Find and write out the subject, verb, object and indirect object in each of the following sentences.

1. The angry policeman gave the cheeky children a final warning.

2. Many hands make light work for everyone.

3. I wrote a long letter to my brother.

4. Every evening, before bed, their father told the little children an exciting story.

5. The teachers have given us too much homework.

EXTENSIONS OF SIMPLE SENTENCES

Find and write out the subject, verb, object – and all extensions – in each of the following sentences.

1. David, trembling with excitement, quickly opened the parcel wrapped in green paper.

2. The angry crowd had chased the wicked thief along the street.

3. Next week, the new recruits will have to sit the more difficult exam.

4. Every morning, the local dairy delivers delicious milk to our house.

5. Have the smaller children managed to complete the whole race across the fields?

COMPLEX SENTENCES

Find and write out the principal and subordinate clauses in each of the following sentences.

1. After the snow had stopped we left the house.

2. Until Mary arrived we could not begin the concert.

3. When you return we shall eat the cake which you made last night.

4. I have discovered the name of the person whose ring was found in the swimming pool.

5. Before Jane moved here she lived in a house which had a leaking roof.

JOINING SENTENCES

Join the following sentences together using conjunctions and relative pronouns (who, whom, which, that, whose).

1. The lorry crashed last night. The lorry was carrying liquid soap. This spread all over the road. There were more accidents. Other vehicles slid out of control.

2. We found the dog. The dog had been run over by a car. We took him to the vet. The vet found no serious injuries.

3. Gardeners usually love to see some rain falling. It helps to make everything grow. Most of us prefer dry, sunny weather.

4. He had tried very hard. The work was still too difficult. Jamie decided to ask for help from his brother. His brother was a maths teacher.

5. Joan has always loved skating. Joan has lessons every week at the ice rink. She wants to enter competitions.

FORMAL AND INFORMAL REGISTER

Hiya! How you doin'? I'm goin' to tell you about writin' formally and informally. Don't get all hot and bothered about it! You'll soon get the hang of it!

This is friendly and chatty language. It uses shortened words and slang expressions like "hang of it".

It is the sort of language we use when we are talking to friends and family. We can use slang and chatty words because we can easily explain anything that is not clear. This is what we call **Informal Register.**

When we are writing about facts and sharing information, it is very important that we make everything clear and exact the first time. We may not be there to explain if the reader does not understand exactly what we meant to write.

Welcome! This section will explain formal and informal writing. It is straightforward and easy to understand.

This version is much less chatty. It uses the full version of each word. It uses words which say exactly what is meant. For instance, no-one is "getting the hang" in this version! This sort of writing, which tries to make sure that there are no misunderstandings, is called **Formal Register.**

WRITING REPORTS IN FORMAL REGISTER

Reports are written in order to give clear, exact information to other people. They should be well organised so they are easy to follow. It is important to make sure there are no misunderstandings.

Successful Reports...

- have a clear title
- explain the purpose in the introduction
- use complete words at all times
- are written in the Third Person
- do not use slang, chatty expressions or dialect
- are written in clear sentences
- are organised in clear paragraphs with topic sentences
- use signal and linking words to guide readers
- use correct spelling and punctuation
- include relevant facts; exclude irrelevant facts

USING SIGNAL (LINKING) WORDS

Signal words help to guide the reader through the report. Each paragraph should have one clear topic. Each sentence should make one clear point. Signal words help to show the direction of the next sentence or paragraph. This might develop the same topic, take a different approach, introduce a new aspect of the subject or change direction completely.

TYPICAL SIGNAL WORDS AND PHRASES

next	furthermore
likewise	in addition
similarly	thus
therefore	consequently
accordingly	as a result
without doubt	yet
on the other hand	however
on the contrary	nevertheless
in spite of	

FIVE POWERFUL SIGNAL WORDS:

such   this   these   those   that

These five signal words link the next sentence or paragraph very strongly to the point which has just been made.

Examples

Every Saturday morning he worked in the charity shop. **Such** kindness was greatly appreciated.

There were not enough seats on the bus so more than twenty members of the club had to stay at home. **These** people were given a refund.

PRACTICE

Read this short report. Try to spot the features of formal writing which make it clear.

Looking After Others in the Cold

The recent wintry weather has caused concern all over the country.

Safety is a priority for everyone. The current advice is to avoid travelling if at all possible. Nevertheless, if they must make a journey, all drivers are advised to watch out for black ice on untreated roads. Black ice can be a dangerous hazard, especially in rural areas. Furthermore, if longer journeys are necessary, it is important to make sure the car is well equipped with warm clothing, blankets and food in case there are more long delays after heavy snowfalls.

In addition, there is concern for the elderly who are particularly at risk in several ways. Icy pavements can cause serious accidents and injuries. For this reason it is often better to stay indoors. It is very important to keep warm: eating at least one hot meal a day helps to prevent hypothermia. Friends and neighbours are therefore encouraged to check on older people, especially those who are living on their own, on a daily basis.

Similarly, parents should warn their children about the dangers of playing on ice-covered ponds. Although the recent cold weather has caused a lot of ponds and lakes to freeze, children should not attempt to skate or slide until the ice has been thoroughly checked by an adult.

This advice has been issued by local government offices throughout Scotland.

SECTION 3:

LANGUAGE

TECHNIQUES

This section explains language techniques that are frequently used for various purposes. We can learn to use them ourselves so that we are able to speak and write more effectively.

Nowadays, when we read, listen or watch any sort of communication, it is also very important to be aware of language techniques and the powerful effects they can have upon our understanding, our opinions and even our behaviour.

A number of short passages have been included for discussion and practice. They demonstrate how language techniques can be employed within several different genres including fiction, reflection, persuasion and travel. The answer section provides fairly detailed comments, for reference.

IMAGERY: FIGURES OF SPEECH

These are arrangements of words which can be used to highlight particular points.

Simile (as...as/like): a figure of speech in which the writer compares what is being described to something else associated with a particular feature. Similes are used to emphasise a special characteristic. His face was as white as snow. He was stubborn, like a mule.

His face was as white as snow. He was stubborn, like a mule.

Metaphor: used in the same way as a simile, to emphasise a special characteristic. The metaphor states or suggests that one thing actually is another.

She was a mouse in the classroom. (timidity)

He was a mountain amongst other men. (huge size)

They galloped and cantered from the classroom. (wild, fast movement)

Personification: in this figure of speech the writer refers to something inanimate as if it is alive and, therefore, has intelligence and feelings.

The storm raged above them; the wind screamed its frustration, clawing at the mast as if determined to pull it from the boat; the waves rose menacingly behind.

Onomatopoeia: the use of words which sound like the noise they describe.

cackle smash babble thud

Alliteration: the use of several words close together which begin with the same letter. Alliteration is used to highlight key words. You should then say why these words are important.

The arrogant, aggressive, abominable creature!

Assonance: another name for rhyming words. It is the use of several words which contain the same vowel sounds. Assonance, like alliteration, is used to emphasise key words and ideas.

fat cats, white light

Irony: the surprising use of opposites or the unexpected. A fireman who commits arson is ironic.

If you lie in your chair while your mother works and she thanks you for your help, she is being ironic.

Sarcasm: the unpleasant tone which often accompanies irony. It combines with irony to make the target feel uncomfortable. Sarcasm is usually bitter and mocking.

You clever fellow! You have slept in again. Your lateness is so reliable!

Euphemism: a way of referring to something unpleasant in more acceptable terms.

die: kick the bucket/pass away

toilet: smallest room

unemployed: between jobs

in prison: staying as a guest of Her Majesty

Hyperbole: the deliberate use of exaggeration, often to create humour or mockery.

Those teachers seem to give us homework to make themselves feel better: they throw worksheets at us like confetti!

Litotes: the opposite of hyperbole. It is the deliberate understatement of a situation. Litotes is used for emphasis and to create humour or mockery.

A cheery Orcadian, holding on to the same lamp-post to avoid being blown away, told me that there was a "bit of a breeze"!

Transferred Epithet: the surprising use of adjectives or adjective phrases which are normally associated with a different topic. In this way the writer can combine two ideas very neatly. Thus, transferred epithets are associated with very vivid, succinct description.

The vengeful, angry punches knocked him to the ground.

Connotative Words: words which carry extra suggestions. We say that particular words "have connotations of…"

The elephant came lumbering towards us, knocking bushes aside on the way.

"Lumbering" describes clumsy movement but it also has connotations of great size and power. Connotative words usually help to create atmosphere, tone or mood.

Juxtaposition: the placing of two surprising words together. The combination will sum up an important point.

*She loves the **delicious torture** of eating red hot peppers.*

THE IMPACT AND EFFECTIVENESS OF VARIOUS SENTENCE STRUCTURES

Writers often use sentence structure to highlight an idea, a mood, an atmosphere or a tone. In this section, consider the purpose of each example.

Short

He returned immediately.

Two minutes later, the bomb exploded.

Then they departed.

Short and Monosyllabic

The storm broke.

I dare you.

Do not go!

Minor (no principal clause)

And again. And again.

As had been expected.

More than ever before.

Because he cares.

Long (with conjunctions, lists, parenthesis, phrases, clauses)

As soon as he entered the room, everyone stopped talking; someone clattered a plate; mouths dropped open; eyes swivelled nervously; a napkin fluttered to the ground as an older woman fainted.

Questions

What should we do next? Where could we go? Who would dare to help us? Who would not betray us?

Rhetorical Questions

Who would want to be known as a racist?

Exclamations

They had arrived! They were two hours too early! We were not ready!

Orders (imperatives)

Sit down! Do not speak to me! Stop shouting! Stop blaming everyone else! Do what I say!

Inverted

Great was our relief when the parents finally departed and we could proceed with our secret party. Even greater was our horror when they returned unexpectedly two hours later. Indescribable was their fury when they saw what was going on.

Repeated Structures

As above: any structure that is repeated increases the impact.

Climactic

In our house my father is the fixer of everything from dripping taps to collapsed computers; he is the peacemaker when we argue and fight; he is usually generous when we need extra pocket money; he provides lifts whenever we need them; in short, he is an excellent dad.

Balanced

To err is human; to forgive is divine.

School term means doing as little as possible; holidays mean doing nothing at all.

Word Position

Writers may choose to place key words at the beginning or end of a sentence.

John walked **reluctantly** to school.

Reluctantly, John walked to school.

John walked to school **reluctantly**.

THE IMPACT OF LISTS

Lists are always used for emphasis. They are the simplest, most dramatic way of developing a point.

In the following examples, we might just have said that someone "bought fruit".

By using various kinds of lists, however, we can make this sound much more important and exciting.

Normal List

He bought fruit: apples, bananas, pears and oranges.

Asyndetic List

He bought fruit: apples, pears, bananas, oranges!

Polysyndetic List

He bought fruit: apples and pears and bananas and oranges!

Giving last item a separate sentence

He bought fruit: apples, pears and bananas. He bought oranges!

Tricolon

This is the name given to a list of three items. It is a famous, ancient technique of emphasis and persuasion used by the great Roman, Cicero, and many other famous orators.

Example

"Government **of the people, by the people, for the people."** (Abraham Lincoln)

PARENTHESIS

Parenthesis is the insertion of extra information to affect meaning.

The most common effects are on **TONE, MOOD** or **ATMOSPHERE** (see separate page).

Parenthesis can usually be spotted with two commas, dashes or brackets separating the basic facts from the extra information.

NOTE

When extra information is placed either at the beginning or end of a sentence, a single dash or a comma is used.

In the following example, we could just stick to the **fact**:

John always won that prize.

Adding some extra words in parenthesis reveals the writer's attitude (**tone**):

John, **with boring regularity**, always won that prize.

John, **the teacher's pet**, always won that prize.

John, **despite having so many troubles**, always won that prize.

John, **to everyone's delight**, always won that prize.

PUNCTUATION

Punctuation marks help to show that a particular sentence structure has been used.

Semi-colon;

A semi-colon separates 2 sentences which are closely linked in purpose or meaning.

Example

Many children walk to school every morning; others ride their bicycles.

Colon:

A colon separates 2 sentences. The first sentence makes a point. The second explains or illustrates that point.

Example

The football match was cancelled this afternoon: the pitch has been flooded again.

Inverted Commas " "

Inverted commas mark words that writers indicate do not belong to them. This may be for various reasons:

- acknowledging someone else's choice of words (quotation)
- slang/dialect
- emphasising differing opinion
- jargon.

NOTE

Italics may be used instead of inverted commas.

LINKAGE

In any text, all sentences and paragraphs should be clearly organised in order: one sentence should lead on neatly to the next until a topic is finished. Then a new paragraph should indicate a change of topic, time or place.

Linkage is the term used to describe devices used by a writer to make sure the next sentence or paragraph moves on very smoothly, logically and clearly from the last one.

A common linkage technique is to begin a new paragraph with a sentence which contains

- a word or phrase which echoes the key idea of the previous paragraph

  and

- a word or phrase which refers to the key idea of this new paragraph.

Other linkage techniques include:

- ending with a question and beginning with the answer
- ending with a key word and beginning with the same word
- using powerful linking words which always refer the reader to an item in the previous sentence or paragraph

Examples: such, these, this, those, that.

Signal Words are often used along with linkage techniques to indicate the next step:

- changing idea, place or time completely
- considering a different point of view
- developing same idea, place or time.

Examples: however, but, nevertheless, furthermore, on the other hand, moreover.

TONE, MOOD AND ATMOSPHERE

TONE is the word we use for the attitude or feelings of the writer. Writers can decide to tell us the basic facts objectively, without personal feelings. However, by adding extra words or using other language techniques writers can be subjective, revealing their attitudes or feelings.

TONING WORDS

Confidence/Assertiveness

of course	without doubt/ doubtlessly
certainly	inclusive use of **we**
obviously	will/shall
in fact	always
indeed	everyone/all

Urgency

must	should
ought	have to

Doubt

could	possibly
might/may	maybe
perhaps	if

Derogatory/Pejorative/ Despising

merely	just
only	purely

Surprise/Awe

even

Distance/Disclaimer

they say/claim

it is said /argued /believed /claimed /suggested

some people

other people

the theory is

Example
Basic Fact

The politicians admitted their mistake.

Basic Fact with Mocking Tone

Incredibly, just this once, **even** the politicians admitted their mistake.

The extra words here have connotations of surprise and mockery.

MOOD is the word used to describe the feelings and attitudes of the characters within a story.

Basic Fact

The family gathered in the hall.

Basic Fact with Excited Mood

Chattering, joking and grinning, the family gathered happily and noisily in the hall.

Here, a listing structure of present participles highlighted the excitement.

ATMOSPHERE is the word used to describe the feelings which are aroused by a place.

Basic Fact

The hall was dark.

Basic Fact with Sinister Atmosphere

The hall was dark with gloomy, ominous shadows in every musty corner.

The writer has added adjectives with connotations of danger and threat to create a sinister atmosphere.

CRITICAL READING

It is important to study any text (spoken, written or visual) as a whole. This is because the full meaning and the effectiveness of the text depend on a series of steps, from the beginning to the end.

Look for:

- **title and subheadings**
- **introduction:** engages reader; establishes main argument
- **topic sentences**
- **linkage**
- **patterns and echoes:** repeated sentence structures, ideas, images
- **key words:** difficult or unusual words which are explained or developed, repeated words, connotative words, emotive words
- **imagery:** metaphors, similes, onomatopoeia etc.
- **emphasis:** repetition, placement of words
- **sentence structure:** lists, repetition, inversion, commands, questions etc.
- **punctuation:** colons, semi-colons, question marks, exclamation marks, inverted commas, italics

- **verbs**: the subjunctive (may/might) suggests doubt; the conditional (could/should/would) suggests disappointment, determination or desire; the imperative (must/will/ought) suggests assertiveness and confidence

- **direct speech**: provides information about the person who spoke: mood, attitude or personality

- **explanations and developments** of key words or points are often found after a colon. Difficult words or ideas are often explained either before they are used or, more usually, immediately afterwards. By including a series of similar words or references to the same idea, a writer will also develop an image, tone, mood or atmosphere

- **parenthesis**: extra information, even just one extra word or phrase, will often tell us more about atmosphere, mood or tone

- **pronouns:** it is normal to stick with first, second or third person throughout. Using the **third person** indicates formal, objective writing. Changing to **first person** suggests personal opinion is being offered and can also urge the reader to agree with the writer's opinion. Using the **second person** emphasises that the writer is addressing the reader directly

- **register:** formal register is used for serious, factual approach; informal register is chatty, friendly or amusing

- **irony:** beware of irony: the opposite of the writer's real meaning. Irony nevertheless is always used to emphasise the writer's real meaning. Do not be misled

- **conclusion:** the conclusion sums up the main points of an argument. Look for repetition of words or ideas from the first paragraph or from elsewhere in the passage.

STRUCTURE

The overall structure of any piece of writing will always help to make the main message clear.

Beginnings should engage the reader and introduce the central concern of the text.

Engaging Beginnings

- Use of **present tense** creates a **sense of immediacy** (it's happening as you read).

- Use of **you** suggests writers are pointing to or speaking directly to the reader.

- Use of **we** suggests that writers are including the reader in their ideas, opinions and events.

- Use of **he, she**, **they** or **it** hides the identity of the characters from the reader. It creates mystery, puzzle or intrigue.

- Use of questions creates suspense and suggests answers may be revealed later.

Conclusions should sum up the central concern of the text.

Effective Conclusions

Writers can use various techniques to highlight and sum up the central concern. Commonly used techniques include:

- Repetition of key words, ideas or images.
- Rhetorical Question: urging the reader to agree with the writer
- Anecdote: a little story which emphasises the central concern.
- Listing Structure

CRITICAL READING

- Treat every text, from a newspaper article to a novel, as **a staircase** which takes the reader up a **series of steps** until, **at the top,** the **message is clear**.
- First step (introduction) should indicate the purpose.
- Next steps build the message.
- Final step (conclusion) should sum up.

There are three aspects of Critical Reading.

Understanding

- Do you understand exactly what the writer has meant?
- Can you express this in your own words?
- Can you extract evidence from the passage to prove this?

Analysis

- Can you define the writer's point here?
- Can you name the techniques used here?
- Can you explain their exact meaning?
- Can you explain how the techniques made this point clear?

- Can you quote appropriately to demonstrate your answer?

Evaluation of a Particular Sentence or Paragraph

- Do you understand the writer's overall purpose (central concern)?
- Can you explain the contribution of this part of the text to the central concern?
- Can you quote appropriately to prove your point?

Three Basic Steps:

1. Read title and introduction very carefully.
2. Use critical reading skills to read whole passage.
3. Write down central concern of passage.

Example

John was the most important member of our group. He was, in fact, a magician who seemed to conjure solutions to our problems with a click of his fingers. He produced the tools we needed like rabbits out of a hat, presenting them with a great flourish of delight. We almost expected him to shout, "Abracadabra!"

Understanding

The central concern of this text is that John is a very helpful member of the team because he is good at solving problems.

Analysis

The writer makes this clear by introducing and then **developing the idea** of John being a magician who made difficult things happen quickly and easily. He used a simile which refers to a magician's trick: "like rabbits out of a hat". This **emphasises that** John found tools easily. He used other words that are associated with a magician's skills: "conjure" means to make something happen as if by magic; "click of the fingers" **suggests** speed and ease; "Abracadabra" is a word which magicians often pretend has magic powers.

Evaluation

In this way the use of magical imagery was **very appropriate** because it made John's efficient problem-solving clear.

EXAMPLES OF EFFECTIVE WRITING

The following short passages provide simple examples of various language techniques and how they can be used for various purposes. The passages and questions can be used for discussion or practical criticism.

Sentence Structure, Imagery and Punctuation

The darkening sky, eerie at midday, showed a storm was on its way. Clouds scudded fast overhead; seagulls shrieked and flew for cover; trees leaned away, like old men, from the rising wind; rubbish tumbled along the street and shot into the air.

Abandoning our trip to the beach, we tried to hurry back to the hotel but had to fight against huge gusts which soon began to carry sharp, stinging hailstones. As we rushed round the corner, Mary grumbled that we should have taken our coats with us but it was too late now: we were all thoroughly drenched!

Lightning cracked.

Stunned and horrified, we saw a blue light streak straight from the heavens into Room 24, on the third floor, Seaview Hotel! An evil sizzling monster had entered the building!

"Our room!" screamed Mary. "It's on fire!"

Sure enough, flames were already licking through the window and a dreadful, red glow filled the sky.

TASKS
1. Give the passage a title.
2. Find examples of the following:

semi-colon	parenthesis
direct speech	alliteration
simile	listing structure
colon	onomatopoeia
metaphor	connotative words

Comment on the effect of each technique on atmosphere or mood.

Kitchen Moods

Jane watched him march away, his face rigid with fury. The door slammed. Then there was total silence.

Her hands were trembling. She glanced round the room hesitantly. Should she sit still; ignore his temper? Should she run after him; beg him to forgive her? Had she been unfair? Was it her fault?

No! Let him go! Let him run back to his mother! Let him behave like the spoiled child he was! She was better off alone!

She stood up fiercely, strode through the kitchen and threw the remains of the steak pie into the dog's dish. She smiled as he gobbled it up.

"Someone likes my cooking after all!"

TASKS

Identify the moods of the characters.

Explain how word choice and sentence structure make these moods clear.

A Worthwhile Journey

Finding the best pizza place in Fiorente is almost impossible – but worth it. In fact, we might suspect that the location is cunningly designed to work up the only sort of appetite that can cope with Signora Adami's menu.

From the harbour, we headed north, up a steep set of steps which were soon shrouded in deep gloom. Shadows grew out from the walls until, despite the midday sun, they met in the middle and seemed to form a tunnel of absolute darkness.

Our guide moved faster round to the right and turned along a narrow alley and climbed up more steps and dodged round more corners and nipped through several gateways and under balconies which dripped white washing and gaudy, fragrant flowers. Gasping with effort (and terror at the thought of being left behind) we followed – for at least half a mile. The "tunnel" opened once more into bright sunlight – and another formidable set of steps.

After that, it was more or less straightforward: we could follow our noses. Who needs a street map when such delicious aromas advertise the way? We arrived ready to enjoy a banquet – and we did!

TASKS

1. Define the main purpose of the text.
2. Explain how the writer uses sentence structure to illustrate the nature of the journey.
3. How does the writer use parenthesis to add humour to the account of the journey?
4. Why has the writer used inverted commas round "tunnel" in paragraph three?
5. Why has the writer used a colon in the final paragraph?
6. In the final paragraph, how does sentence structure emphasise the writer's meaning?

NOTE

Questions 2 and 6 are useful examples of the sort of question which requires you to define the writer's meaning, before evaluating the effectiveness of the sentence structure in making it clear.

A Happy Surprise

The local school was a drab old-fashioned building: the doors and windows were flaking paint; the stones of the walls were black with soot. The bleak edifice towered ominously over the empty miserable playground like a grim policeman, warning against any childish fun or joy.

Yet, just as crusty human exteriors often disguise warm and kindly hearts, first impressions of this formidable structure belied the startling welcome inside: tiny tots who quavered through the massive doors on their first day found themselves surrounded by bright, rainbow-coloured walls and floors and doors; nursery rhyme characters were depicted on every available space; toys and games and cuddly toys were stacked round every corner.

And then there were the teachers and helpers: even if the outside walls glowered balefully at the new recruits the staff welcomed them cheerily with reassuring smiles.

TASKS

1. Define the main purpose of the text.
2. Evaluate the effectiveness of
   - overall structure
   - development of ideas
   - sentence structure
   - linkage
   - punctuation

DEVELOPING IDEAS

Writers often introduce an idea and then develop
their argument by using more words and imagery
associated with the same idea. Sometimes they will
even repeat key words.

Example

His anger finally emerged. He started to behave like a
wild, ferocious dog. His lips leered back over his
teeth; his hackles rose; drawing himself up as if about
to go in for the kill, he snarled a warning to the other
man. Suddenly he pounced, full of murder.

FEELING THE HEAT

Each morning the sun rose like a furnace in the sky, just after five o'clock. Thereafter, the relentless roasting of the earth continued till nightfall. For some the heat was altogether too intense: wilting and withering, they remained in our air-conditioned hotel, sheltering from the blast and, in just one week, spent their entire holiday budget on ice-cold drinks.

But we were made of sterner stuff and, in the afternoon of our second day, we walked along the promenade to the harbour and the village. All of the inhabitants must have retired to their siesta: not a soul was in sight. The swathes of empty golden sand and the sleepy silence were quite unnerving; a caravan of camels and desert tribesmen would not have surprised us at all. Shimmering, as in a mirage, the bright hulls and masts of countless little fishing boats eventually emerged from the haze.

Postcard pretty this scene may have been but, after ten minutes walking in such heat, we were driven, by basic instincts of survival, to move on quickly to the nearest oasis – a tiny little café at the end of the pier – where we quenched our thirst with glasses of exotically flavoured (iced) tea.

TASKS

1. Define the writer's main purpose.
2. In terms of the writer's main purpose, evaluate the effectiveness of the following techniques:

- imagery
- word choice
- irony
- structure

BULLYING

It seems fairly obvious, from literature and from history, that bullying – the subjugation by torment of one person by another – has been accepted as a common feature of British society for a very long time.

Some of our finest public schools appear to have incorporated and accommodated bullying within their ranks of staff and pupils as an informal aspect of their much vaunted "character building" ethos. Captains of industry and government have been applauded for their determination, conviction and ruthless decisiveness. Until quite recently, very few questions had been asked about the less desirable effects of such behaviour and the social values it represents.

Nowadays, however, the bully in the workplace, the playground and even at home has become the focus of intense debate and apparent concern. Furthermore, a superficial glance at newspaper headlines and political statements might suggest that the national approach is a clear, simple matter of condemnation and recompense: "zero tolerance" some might claim.

Simple condemnation? Nothing could be further from my recent experience in a local office. Reduced to a shivering, nervous jelly of apprehension, I was instructed to "consider the bully's personal difficulties" and to "assess my own contribution to the situation". This outrageous and impossible suggestion culminated in a gruesome and ridiculous confrontation during which a well-meaning – but misguided – human resources officer invited me to "understand and move forward" with my tormentor.

What?

I declined her offer. Shortly afterwards, however, I did indeed "move forward" to a promoted post as manager in a different company.

Yesterday, with conviction and ruthless decisiveness, I sacked an employee for bullying a colleague.

Zero tolerance? Absolutely!

TASKS

1. Define the main purpose of the text.

2. Discuss the structure of the whole passage.

3. In terms of the writer's main idea, evaluate the effectiveness of the following:

   - word choice
   - imagery
   - sentence structure
   - punctuation
   - tone
   - linkage
   - conclusion

THE HOUSE ON THE HILL

1. As children, we were fascinated by the chimneys which occasionally belched smoke over the tops of the trees on Harrier Hill. They teased and tantalised our curiosity; we were drawn relentlessly; we peered and guessed wildly. But the chimneys were all we could ever see of the house without trespassing. Inevitably, of course, we risked a lot of that.

2. There were various ways in which uninvited guests could enter the grounds. Our usual route was through the gnarled old forsythia bush which nestled against the high wall just beyond the church. A couple of branches up from the ground, we transferred to well-worn toeholds in the mortar, scrambled over the top and swung on to a knotted rope slung from the branch of a huge oak tree. We landed on ground soft with moss and bracken. Beyond these ancient trees there was a deep jungle of rhododendron: a perfect landscape for our eager imaginations and hunger for adventure.

3. Within this dark, enticing wilderness, one apparently impenetrable bush had been chosen as our den. Here vast tentacles of mangled rhododendron spread in a wide circle; a massive dome of thick glossy greenery prohibited access; it appeared inviolate, intact. However, behind a particularly heavy frond which swept the ground, we had established a wriggling, scrabbling desperately secret route to the centre. Initiation to our gang was marked by a novice's first visit; knowledge of the

den was the ultimate privilege: a mark of status, in our opinion, beyond royalty.

4. Although the large stone gateposts had been carved with what must have been the original owner's choice of name, "Woodburn", everyone in the village referred to it as the "house on the hill". In fact, the whole family seemed to come under this title. I remember how gossip would note that the "house on the hill" had gone for the summer; it had left for an important wedding in London; it was clearly expecting important visitors: the gates had been painted again.

5. When the chauffeur delivered a weekend grocery order to the village shop, Mr. Hinchley never seemed to mention Mrs. Mansfield. Moustache bristling with urgency, he flourished her list and barked, "Fill that box for the house on the hill!"

6. His other, ordinary customers, abandoned, would quietly step aside in awe: aware of the moment. The assistants scurried anxiously around, distracted by the demands of perfect service: the house on the hill, with its chimneys, expected no less.

7. Maybe that is why, a lifetime later, when I returned to my little Yorkshire village, it was so important and so marvellous to look up from the main street and discover that the chimneys were still there, poking their heads over the heavy summer foliage of beech, ash and oak. They were symbols of so much that had happened, so many adventures, so much happiness, so many dearly loved friends...

TASKS

1. What is the main idea of this passage?

2. In paragraph 1, how does the writer use word choice, sentence structure and punctuation to create a vivid impression of the children's curiosity?

3. Comment on the effectiveness of linkage between paragraphs 2 and 3.

4. In paragraph 3, how does the writer's use of language develop the idea of wilderness?

5. In paragraph 4, show how the author develops the idea that all the villagers saw the house as an important feature of their lives.

6. In paragraphs 5 and 6, how does the writer develop the importance of the "house on the hill"?

7. In paragraph 7 what separate techniques does the writer use to indicate that a great deal of time has passed since his childhood?

In the beautifully structured passage which follows, the travel writer, Jan Morris, describes her impressions of Aberdeen in the early 1980s.

OIL ON GRANITE

1. For my tastes, the harbour of Aberdeen is marvellous to see in the evening. It is not a big harbour, two artificial inlets attached to the mouth of the Dee and protected by a breakwater against the open sea, but it is always in motion. The rusty flotillas of fishing boats may be asleep, their blur of masts and funnels illuminated only by a few masthead lights, but the oil docks all around are brilliantly awake. The tall storage tanks glitter in the floodlights. The ungainly supply-boats, humped up forward, elongated aft, hum at their quays. From the shrouded shape of a vessel in the yards, towered over by derricks, a fireworks spray of oxy-acetylene showers through the dusk.

2. There are hissing, clanging and thumping noises; the pilot launch scuds here and there; the hulk of a freighter heaves itself cautiously from a quay; the Orkney steamer slips away down the navigation channel, exchanging incomprehensible Scotticisms with the harbour-men in their tower. Out at sea, four or five supply boats lie beneath their riding lights, and sometimes a helicopter comes clanking in from the east, heavily over the docks towards the airport.

3.   Aberdeen is the chief support base for the North Sea oil operations. Here are the supply-ships, the depots, the aircraft, the electronics, the technical agencies which sustain the storm-battered rigs and platforms far out at sea. Thousands of millions of pounds are invested in these craft and machineries; skills from a dozen nations are concentrated here; through this conduit, Americans, Englishmen, Frenchmen, Dutchmen, Spaniards, Italians, Greeks, Norwegians, Swedes, Germans pass in a ceaseless traffic to and from the oilfields out of sight.

4.   Yet behind the harbour, as night falls, the city of Aberdeen stands grave and grey. A tower or two, of kirk or civic pile, stand sentinel beyond the cranes, like keepers of the public conscience, but there are no skyscrapers, revolving restaurants on towers, neon lights or blazing late-night stores. No thump of disco echoes down Mill Brae or Rennie's Wynd. Aberdeen seems hardly more than a backdrop to the performance on its own quays for, though this old and respected burgh has long joined the list of boom towns, Kimberley to Abu Dhabi, it remains tentative to the experience. Other towns have gold rushes or silver strikes: Aberdeen's is a strictly granite bonanza.

5.   Handsome, civilised, diligent, granite, Aberdeen has never been rich before, but has always been canny. Until the oil strikes, it lived by fishing and agriculture and, though it knew much poverty and unemployment in the bad old days, it never let its standards slip. Its very substance seemed indestructible, so that its buildings never looked

old or new, never particularly shabby, never noticeably opulent.

6. It is very hard to date a building in Aberdeen, so easily does one century blend into the next. The grandest houses in town, the severe granite villas built for the trawler owner at the turn of the century, are scarcely ostentatious: the old fishing quarter of Footdee, jumbled on the shore beside the harbour, is still occupied by fishing families and dockyard workers but has been done up bijou-style by the council, with concrete bowls for shrubberies and dainty cobbled yards.

7. This city of 200,000 lies halfway between Edinburgh and John O'Groats. Here the produce of the eastern Highlands traditionally comes to market; here the fish of the north are frozen, whisked away to London or turned into malodorous by-products. Aberdeen is deeply rooted.

8. Little has really changed since the 18th century, I would imagine, at the auction by which, each morning at 8am, the trawlers dispose of their catch. The boats, rimmed still with frost and ice from the fishing grounds, mostly look antique themselves and the fishermen look altogether timeless, stalwart, comely men, their faces rigid in the truest Scottish mould, unhurried, polite; and there the fish of the cold seas lie as they always did: cod, hake and flatfish, glistening in their wooden crates. Through all the hub-bub - the slithering of seaboots, the clattering of boxes, the chugging of engines, the shrieking of seabirds, the slurping of tea from enamel mugs - white-coated

auctioneers immemorially grunt their prices and lorries rumble away over the cobbled quays.

9. It is an interesting but not an exhilarating scene, but then Aberdeen is not built for exuberance. It is not, as one of its inhabitants remarked to me, a *fizzy* town.

10. The crime rate is the lowest, as are the juvenile delinquency rate and the vandalism rate and the unemployment rate: and the educational standards are the highest and the long beach promenade is entirely unvulgarised and the town has won the Britain in Bloom contest so often that it has tactfully withdrawn from the contest. Aberdeen has an enterprising arts centre, municipally supported, and its high-rise buildings have been tastefully held in check and its industrial development is discreetly zoned and altogether it is in many ways the best of all possible burghs.

11. Upon this hoary and provident town the bonanza of oil has fallen more or less out of the sky. Until I went to Aberdeen I had no conception of its scale. Seen against so stolid a setting, it is staggering. One oil person actually apologised to me for a development that cost a mere million: anything less than a billion or two is hardly worth mentioning. There is nothing modest to the North Sea oil affair.

12. It is like a war and billeted upon Aberdeen, as alien to the city as the officers of some occupying army, are the staffs and technical corps of the campaign. This is the intelligence base of the North Sea operations, the logistical centre, the technical depot; here too are all the auxiliaries:

financiers to camp followers, landladies to economists. The local oil directory lists them all and their very entries on the page are like a roll-call of regiments, drawn from all corners of some great alliance and assembled beneath their several flags in this unlikely outpost.

13. But there is beauty here. It is the beauty of power and innovation, which inspired the artist Turner in his day but is hard to find in modern Britain. It is the brutal beauty of competitive enterprise: men racing each other, the snatch for profit, the outpouring of colossal resources in the hope of still more immense returns. It suits this hard northern coastline, where the wild storms sweep in from the sea and where once the Aberdeen clippers sailed out to capture the prizes of the tea trade. Oil tycoons may have their doubts about London, even about Edinburgh, but they can hardly quarrel with Aberdeen.

OIL ON GRANITE QUESTIONS

The central concern of this passage is the author's admiration of two aspects of the city of Aberdeen: the complexity and huge size of the oil industry and the strength of the traditional culture of the city. She argues that the old city copes very well with the arrival of the oil industry.

1. In paragraph 1, comment on the effectiveness of the sentence structure in sentences 2 and 3.

2. How does the writer develop the idea of the harbour being "brilliantly awake"?

3. In paragraph 2, by referring to the writer's use of language, show how she creates a vivid impression of noise and movement in the harbour.

4. In paragraph 3, with particular reference to sentence structure, show how the writer develops her point that Aberdeen is the centre of the North Sea Oil industry.

5. In paragraph 4, show how the writer indicates a change of theme.

6. In the same paragraph, by referring to word choice, sentence structure and imagery, show how she makes it clear that Aberdeen has reacted very cautiously to the arrival of the oil industry.

7. Comment on the effectiveness of the link between paragraph 4 and paragraph 5.

8. Which aspect of Aberdeen does the writer introduce in paragraph 5 as a symbol of the fact

that Aberdeen has not changed much throughout history?

9. In paragraph 6 how does the writer develop her use of this symbol – making it a vehicle for her argument that Aberdeen has strong traditions?

10. In paragraph 7, how does the writer develop her theme of tradition?

11. In paragraph 8, which part of Aberdeen does the writer now use to develop the idea of tradition?

12. By discussing her use of language show how the writer creates a vivid sense of place and history in this paragraph.

13. In paragraph 9, comment on the effect of the writer's use of the words "exhilarating", "exuberance", and "fizzy". How do they contribute to the overall argument of the passage?

14. Why has she written *fizzy* in italics?

15. In paragraph 10 show how the writer has used sentence structure, word choice and other techniques to make her meaning clear.

16. In paragraph 11, with reference to word choice and other language techniques, show how the author brings her two main ideas together.

17. In paragraph 12, by discussing the writer's use of imagery and other language techniques, show how she emphasises the huge impact of the oil industry on Aberdeen.

18. With reference to the writer's central concern, her two contrasting themes and her use of language techniques, show how paragraph 13 is an effective conclusion to this article.

ABOUT THE AUTHOR

Frances McKie, MA   DipEd, taught English in various schools in Scotland from 1974 to 2014. She believes in the importance of giving everyone the chance to take command of their own language and to experience all the advantages and empowerment this will bring.

ANSWER SCHEME

Page 6: Verbs Nouns Adjectives

1. We change into **play** clothes when we come home from school. **Adjective**
2. I lost a **shoe** on the beach. **Noun**
3. They **dress** smartly on Sunday. **Verb**
4. John tidied everything into the **toy** cupboard. **Adjective**
5. The children **play** happily in the park. **Verb**
6. We have moved to a new **house**. **Noun**
7. Mum cooked a huge pie for our **house** guests. **Adjective**
8. The blacksmith will **shoe** all the horses before he leaves. **Verb**
9. You can buy new boots at the **shoe** shop. **Adjective**
10. She bought a blue **dress** for the party. **Noun**
11. Cats often **toy** with the mice that they catch. **Verb**
12. We enjoyed watching an exciting **play** at the theatre. **Noun**
13. Dad built a big hutch and we **house** the rabbits in that. **Verb**
14. They love to wander round the **dress** shops on Saturdays. **Adjective**
15. That ball is Jill's favourite **toy**. **Noun**

Page 9: Nouns

street	town	policemen
house	dog	police
walls	garden	people
cars	policeman	handcuffs
gate	motorbike	building
ladies	radio	criminals
man	van	
vehicles	kerb	

Page 12: Plural Nouns

eggs	teeth	houses
months	cases	geese
stories	quays	mummies
diaries	dollies	families
men	mice	daddies
desks	lions	brothers
buses	feet	lorries

Page 17: Apostrophe

John entered the **headmaster's** office. He gave his boss the lists of pupils who had taken part in the expedition and began to explain what had happened.

"All the teams were supposed to meet at the bridge and hike to the campsite together. **Peter's** rucksack was too heavy and **he'd** given some heavy water bottles to the others to carry for him. They **hadn't** minded at first but it **wasn't** long before they were all complaining. The younger **boys'** voices were loudest because they were exhausted. Our leaders soon decided **we'd** do better to set up the tents two miles from the campsite. **That's** when things became really disastrous."

Page 19: Proper Nouns

Edinburgh	primary school	government
football	House of Commons	cooker
horse	Central Primary School	cupboard
market	elephant	High Street
Scotland	European Parliament	
policeman	university	
Atlantic Ocean	Hampden Football Stadium	

Page 20: Collective Nouns

a library of books	a set of tools
a class of pupils	a choir of singers
a gaggle or skein of geese	a chest of drawers
a pack of wolves	a bouquet of flowers
a kit or flock of pigeons	a constellation of stars
a gang of thieves	a flight of stairs
a team of footballers	a school or pod of
a flock of birds	whales
a regiment of soldiers	a swarm of bees
a murder of crows	a troop of monkeys
a parliament or party of	a crowd of people
politicians	a pride of lions
an orchestra of musicians	a quiver of arrows
a litter of puppies	a punnet of strawberries
a fleet of ships	a bunch of bananas

Page 24: Persons of the Verb

(I) remember - First	(we) were going - First
(we) went - First	(I) was walking- First
(teacher) taught - Third	(boys) started to jostle - Third
(she) organised - Third	
(we) could read - First	(you) are- Second
(children) felt -Third	(they) yelled- Third
(they) teased - Third	(Tam) ran- Third
(they) shouted - Third	(he) did not come- Third

Page 34: Finding Verbs

(I) remember: First Person, Singular, Present Tense

(we) had been hoping to hire: First Person, Plural, Past Pluperfect Tense

(we) arrived: First Person, Plural, Past Perfect Tense

(the manager) gave: Third Person, Singular, Past Perfect Tense

(he) promised: Third Person, Singular, Past Perfect Tense

(we) paid: First Person, Plural, Past Perfect Tense

(we) could use: First Person, Plural, Conditional

(we) were eating: First Person, Plural, Past Imperfect

(someone) knocked: Third Person, Singular, Past Perfect Tense

(David) opened: Third Person, Singular, Past Perfect Tense

(he) shouted: Third Person, Singular, Past Perfect Tense

(our neighbours) had arrived: Third Person, Plural, Past Pluperfect Tense

(they) had spotted: Third Person, Plural, Past Pluperfect Tense

they) walked: Third Person, Plural, Past Perfect Tense
(we) spent: First Person, Plural, Past Perfect Tense
(the weather) was: Third Person, Singular, Past
Perfect Tense
(we) enjoyed: Third Person, Plural, Past Perfect Tense
(we) are: First Person, Plural, Present Tense
(we) might go: First Person, Plural, Subjunctive Mood

Page 38: Adjectives

most beautiful: superlative	lonely: positive
many: positive	happiest: superlative
lovely: positive	elder: comparative
charity: positive	younger: comparative
excellent: positive	gentle: positive
better: comparative	stronger: comparative
old: positive	worse: comparative
tiny: positive	

Page 44: Prepositions

across the platform	in his wallet
with both hands	on the kitchen table
into the carriage	inside her own purse
on her lap	after a moment
along the corridor	in his little black book
at home	

Page 46: Co-ordinating Conjunctions

Johnny **and** Peter	**and** joins two proper names
excited **but** nervous	**but** joins two adjectives
they wanted to reach the top...**so** they travelled	**so** joins two sentences
clothing **and** food	**and** joins two nouns
Johnny had completed...**and** he was lowering	**and** joins two sentences
up **or** down	**or** joins two adverbs
it was not possible to pull...**so** Johnny climbed down to release it	**so** joins two sentences
he slipped **and** grabbed	**and** joins two verbs
he slipped **and** grabbed...**but** he became tangled in the rope	**but** joins two sentences
trapped **and** left	**and** joins two past participles
Peter climbed up to help **but** he could not reach Johnny	**but** joins two sentences
the rope broke... **and** Johnny fell to the bottom	**and** joins two sentences
he explained... **so** a helicopter was sent	**so** joins two sentences

Page 59: Participles

These are the correct sentences. Each sentence has a complete verb and a subject.

1. **The snow was falling** heavily in the wood.
2. **The children had sung** several beautiful songs.
3. Having tidied the room **we switched** off the lights.
4. **We were driving** fast along the motorway on a very warm day.
5. Annoyed by the flies, **the poor horse had been swishing** his tail to keep them away.

Page 62: Subject and Verb

Subject	Verb
The horses	had been galloping
Peter	was sleeping
The ships	will be sailing
Jane	would have liked to sing
I	have arrived

Page 65: Subject Verb and Object

Subject	Verb	Object
The girls	had been playing	tennis
Peter	loves to eat	sausage and chips
We	would like to see	your holiday photographs
They	have eaten	too much chocolate.
You	might have tried to clean	that awful mess
The storm	has wrecked	all the tents

Page 65: Subject, Verb and Object

Subject	Verb	Object
The whole class	has visited	the museum
They	ought to have come	
I	would love to watch	that film
They	are resting	
He	must have been running	
They	have collected	all the rubbish
The crowd	rushed	
Many people	have climbed	that mountain
The bus	is running	
I	would love to eat	the whole cake

Page 68: Verb, Subject, Object and Indirect Object

Subject	Verb	Object	Indirect Object
He	has given	a beautiful bunch of flowers	me
Jane	had baked	a delicious cake	(for) her friend
I	used to send	a birthday card	her
They	must buy	some new boots	Peter
His father	bought	that amazing car	him
John	will have to post	that parcel	(for)dad
I	explained	the situation	(to) him
The policeman	gave	a warning	that driver

Page 69: Indirect Object

1. On his birthday, we brought **John** his favourite doughnuts.
2. The school provided smart football jerseys **for the team**.
3. After the storm neighbours repaired the fence **for the old couple**.
4. Mr Smith sent **the council** an angry letter about litter.
5. They built a flat above the garage **for their elderly parents**.
6. The rich landowner gave a whole field **to the village**.
7. Their mum loves to read **the twins** a story every night at bedtime.
8. At the start of the lesson, the teacher showed **us** the new formula.

Page 70: Question Structure

Subject	Verb	Object
They	did enjoy	the party
You	have finished	your homework
You	would like to buy	this house
John	has forgotten	his coat
I	should have locked	the door

Page 73: Phrases

Subject	Verb	Phrases
The clever collie dog	guided	rounding them up, over the hill, into the shed
The crowd	marched	after the meeting, with great excitement, along the road
John	looked	in the very hot sun, as cool as a cucumber
Peter	scored	kicking the ball, over the goalkeeper's head
Their suitcases	sat	packed with holiday clothes, in a row, beside the door

Page 76: Phrases and Extensions

Subject	Extension of Subject	Verb	Extension of Verb	Object	Extension of Object
the servants	hard-working	had cleaned	early that morning, very thoroughly	the house	old, rambling
the old lady	rushing down the street, old	dropped	suddenly	her bag	huge
my dad	poor old	crashed	yesterday, accidentally, into a tree, outside our house	his car	brand, new
bees	huge	have been appearing	throughout the summer, in our garden		
John	tired and hungry	reached	finally, just before dark	the camp-site	remote

Page 76: Extensions: More Practice

Subject	Verb	Object	Indirect Object
The ship	left	the harbour	
James	scored	the goal	
The couple	decided to buy	the house	
Her neighbour	brought	food	the lady
The family	enjoy	a holiday	
The burglar	entered	the house	
The survivor	told	his story	the reporters
The waves	struck	the pier	

Page 80: Punctuation

1. Jane works very hard; she also plays lots of sports.
2. Edinburgh is a very beautiful city: elegant buildings line many streets; the castle stands high on a huge rock.
3. John will not be coming to the party: he must finish his homework.
4. Are you really going to eat all those cakes? Put them back immediately!
5. The storm broke: rain pelted the streets; trees bent right over in the wind; rubbish flew high in the air.
6. Mary apologised for missing the meeting: she had been stuck in a traffic jam.
7. We are very fond of fruit pies for dessert; we also love ice cream.

8. There were many beautiful trees in the wood: rowan, beech and birch all glowed in the autumn light.

Page 87: Complex Sentences

1. Although you shouted at me I still love you.
2. Because he has arrived late he has missed lunch.
3. Until John leaves school next year he will work hard.
4. Since Mary moved house she has been very happy.
5. After they enjoyed a large supper they went to bed.
6. As you have worked so well you can go home now.
7. We are going to be very late unless the train speeds up.
8. Before we drove off to London that morning Mary fell down the stairs.

Page 95/97: Principal Clause, Subordinate Clause, Subordinating Conjunctions

Principal Clause	Subordinate Clause	Subordinating Conjunction
I will not go	unless you come with me	unless
Jane screamed	when the door opened	when
I do not earn much money	although I work hard	although
we could not light a fire	because the wood was so damp	because
they met their neighbours in the same resort	while the Browns were on holiday in Spain	while
I was reading a book quietly	before they arrived	before
Mary led the walking group	since she knew the area very well	since
Mum always listens to the radio	while she drives to work	while
I will not come	until you invite me	until
we discovered her handbag under a chair	after the visitor left	after

Page 98 Subordinate Relative Clauses

1. The house **that they bought** was very large.
2. The boy **whose ball I lost** was angry.
3. The sweets **which are in the dish** are delicious.
4. The lady **who won the lottery** is my neighbour.
5. Jane and Peter **whom I know very well** are

going to be married.

6. John **whose father plays football for Scotland** is a pupil at our school.

7. I hope to finish the marathon **which is a huge challenge**.

8. People **who take regular exercise** are thought to be healthier.

9. The book **that Mary read** was recommended by her teacher.

10. We booked the hotel **which was given five stars by the tourist board.**

Page 100 Identifying Clauses

Principal Clause	Subordinate Clause	Subordinating Conjunction	Subordinate Relative Clause	Relative Pronoun
John gave a huge sigh of relief	when we reached the station	when	who was carrying the heaviest bags	who
He intends to visit the shopkeeper	because it has never worked properly	because	who sold us the computer	who
Jean buys her plants from these suppliers	as they have a good reputation	as	who loves her garden	who
Peter has had to work very hard	since he returned to school / because he has missed so much classwork	since / because		
The first disaster happened	when they forgot the rucksack	when	that contained all the food	that
we visited the old station café	after we left the train	after	which had been modernised	which
I opened my umbrella	because it started to rain	because	which was immediately ripped by the strong wind	which
the small children behaved like professionals	although they were extremely excited / while they performed on the stage	although / while	whose parents sat in the audience	whose

Page 105 Making Sentences

1. James, **who** is a very clever boy, hopes to become a vet **but** Jane, **who** is very athletic, wants to be a gymnast.
2. **Because** they had slept in, they ran all the way **but** the bus **which** they had been hoping to catch had already gone.
3. Do not be late for tea **as** your friends will be here

176

and the chips **which** you love to eat will be spoiled.

4. **When** the swimming lesson started Jane, **who** was terrified of drowning, refused to enter the water **and** Peter stupidly pushed her into the pool **because** he wanted to have fun.

5. **Since** they were going on holiday they cancelled the papers **but** they forgot to cancel the milk **which** piled up on their doorstep.

Page106 Identifying Clauses

Principal Clauses	Co-ordinating Conjunction	Subordinate Clause	Subordinating Conjunction	Subordinate Relative Clause	Relative Pronoun
1) he could go to college 2) he might decide to work on his father's farm	or	after Peter leaves school	after		
1) Mary turned on the oven 2) it was still cold	but	before she started baking when the cakes were ready to cook	before when		
1) The bus was very late 2) James ordered a taxi	so	because the weather was stormy	because	which arrived very quickly	which
1) we used to go camping every summer 2) now we can afford to stay in hotels 3) I am very happy about that	but and	because it is a cheap form of holiday	because		
1) John started to hoover the stairs 2) he was interrupted by the phone call	but	after he had cleaned the bathroom	after	which he had been expecting	which
1) Mrs Grant walked slowly 2) she missed the bus	so	because she was feeling poorly old	because	which would have taken her to the hospital	which
1) there will be a very poor harvest 2) local farmers will lose a great deal of money	and	unless we have a lot more rain soon	unless	who depend on these crops	who
1) they lived in Edinburgh 2) they have now moved to London	but	before they were married	before	which is a much bigger city.	which

178

Page 109

Revision

Subject, Verb, Object and Indirect Object

Subject	Verb	Object	Indirect Object
The angry policeman	gave	a final warning	the cheeky children
Many hands	make	light work	for everyone.
I	wrote	a long letter	to my brother
Their father	told	an exciting story	the little children
The teachers	have given	too much homework	us

Simple Sentences with Extensions

Subject	Extension of Subject	Verb	Extension of Verb	Object	Extension of Object
David	trembling with excitement	opened	quickly	the parcel	wrapped in green paper
The crowd	angry	had chased	along the street	the thief	wicked
the recruits	new	will have to sit	next week	the exam	more difficult
the dairy	local	delivers	every morning to our house	milk	delicious
the children	smaller	have managed to complete	across the fields	the race	whole

Principal Clause	Subordinate Clause	Subordinating Conjunction	Subordinate Relative Clause	Relative Pronoun
we left the house	after the snow had stopped	after		
we could not begin the concert	until Mary arrived	until		
we shall eat the cake	when you return	when		
we shall eat the cake			which you made last night	which
I have discovered the name of the person			whose ring was found last night	whose
she lived in a house	before Jane moved here	before	which had a leaking roof	which

Page 110   Joining Sentences Together

1. The lorry which crashed last night was carrying liquid soap and this spread all over the road so there were more accidents when other vehicles slid out of control.
2. After we found the dog that had been run over by a car we took him to the vet who found no serious injuries.
3. Although most of us prefer dry, sunny weather, gardeners usually love to see some rain falling because it helps to make everything grow.
4. After he had tried very hard the work was still too difficult so Jamie decided to ask for help from his brother who was a maths teacher.
5. Joan has always loved skating and she has lessons every week at the ice rink because she wants to enter competitions.

Page 140   Sentence Structure, Imagery and Punctuation

- This passage offers a vivid description of an approaching storm.
- The first sentence **sets the scene**.
- "eerie at midday": the **parenthesis** highlights the **connotations** of supernatural in "eerie" and **creates a sinister atmosphere**.
- "Clouds scudded fast…into the air": the **listing structure of sentences**, separated by **semi-colons**, emphasises the many signs of approaching storm.
- "shrieked": **onomatopoeia** suggests fear.

- "like old men": the **simile** of old age and frailty emphasises the destructive force of the wind.
- "tumbled" and "shot": the **connotations** of violence indicate the growing power of the wind.
- "fight against huge gusts": the **connotations** of a struggle confirm the storm is fierce.
- "sharp, stinging hailstones": the **alliteration** highlights violence of the hail and wind.
- "It was too late now: we were all thoroughly drenched!": the **colon** introduces the explanation of why it was "too late" which adds to picture of extreme weather.
- "Lightning cracked": the **short sentence, single sentence paragraph and onomatopoeia** create a climax as storm arrives.
- "stunned and horrified": the **word choice,** describing emotions, creates fearful **mood** and indicates disaster will follow.
- "flames were licking": the **personification** develops the sinister mood of malicious intent.
- "blue light streak straight": the **monosyllables and alliteration** emphasise **dramatic impact** of the lightning strike.
- "evil, sizzling monster": the **personification of lightning,** with malicious intent, and the **onomatopoeia** add to the sinister atmosphere.
- "Our room!" screamed Mary. "It's on fire!": the **direct speech** reveals Mary's panic and creates a fearful mood.
- "screamed": this word conveys terror and develops **fearful mood**; it brings the description of a violent, destructive storm to a **climax.**

Page 141: KITCHEN MOODS

The husband's mood is angry:

"rigid": has **connotations** of being gripped by strong feeling.
"fury": confirms extreme anger.
"slammed": suggests violence.

Jane's mood at the beginning is nervous and uncertain:

"trembling": **suggests** fear and distress.
"hesitantly": has **connotations of** uncertainty and nervousness.
The **listing structure** of **6 questions** emphasises her **uncertainty** and **lack of confidence**.

Jane's mood changes to confidence and decisiveness:

"No!": the **single word** and **exclamation mark** highlight **change of mood** to **decisiveness** and **confidence**.
 The **listing structure** of **3 commands** emphasises **assertive mood**.
"fiercely": indicates **determination** and **aggression**.
"strode": has **connotations** of **confidence** and **decisiveness**.

"smiled": indicates **calm, pleasure** and **satisfaction**.

Page 142: A WORTHWHILE JOURNEY

The main purpose/central concern is a vivid description of a difficult journey on foot.

The sentence structure emphasises difficult nature of journey.

"Our guide moved faster round to the right and turned along a narrow alley and climbed up more steps and dodged round more corners and nipped through several gateways and under balconies which dripped white washing and gaudy, fragrant flowers."

The **polysyndetic list** of varied verbs- "turned", "dodged" and "nipped"- emphasises the many changes of direction and other challenges during the journey.

"Gasping with effort (and terror at the thought of being left behind)":

The **parenthesis** highlights the author's **hyperbolic description** of the uncertainty of the group as "terror". The **exaggeration** of their unnecessary alarm creates humour.

Inverted Commas

Inverted commas are placed round "tunnel" to acknowledge that this is a reference to the writer's earlier use of the word as a metaphor for the shadowy streets.

Use of Colon

The colon in the final paragraph separates the first sentence from the second to show that the second

185

sentence **explains why** the journey was now "straightforward".

Sentence Structure in Final Paragraph

In the final paragraph the writer emphasises that the food they bought in the café was delicious.

"Who needs a street map when such delicious aromas advertise the way?"
This **rhetorical question** highlights the idea of **enticing smells** introduced in the previous sentence.

"We arrived ready to enjoy a banquet – and we did!"
The **dramatic pause before three monosyllabic words** at the end of the sentence creates **a climax** which emphasises that the food was so delicious it was worth the difficult journey.

Page 144: A HAPPY SURPRISE

The main purpose of the passage is to argue that, despite a dreary external appearance, this school was a wonderful place for little children.

Structure

The **first** idea is **negative**: the unpleasant external appearance of the building. The **second** idea is **positive**: the warm interior and the friendly staff. The overall structure is **negative to positive**. In this way the **contrast** and the **structure** emphasise the writer's central concern that this school was a wonderful place for young children.

Development of Negative Idea: Word Choice and Imagery

"drab": **connotations** of ugliness and being worn-out.

"old-fashioned": **suggests** a lack of modern facilities.

"flaking point": **continues idea** of being worn-out, poorly maintained.

"black with soot": **connotations** of dirtiness.

"bleak": **suggests unpleasantness**, a depressing effect on children.

"ominously": **connotations** of danger.

"miserable": **suggests** building makes the **atmosphere unhappy** for everyone.

"like a grim policeman": the **simile** develops negative idea of **oppression: policeman** is a symbol of the law.

"grim" has **connotations** of severity and meanness

Development of Positive Idea: Word Choice and Imagery

"warm and kindly hearts": introduces **contrasting image** of friendliness

"startling welcome inside": the reference to surprise emphasises **the contrast** with the bleak atmosphere outside.

"bright, rainbow-coloured": this cheerful imagery creates a **direct contrast** with "drab".

"nursery rhyme characters": this reference creates a **light-hearted atmosphere;** it suggests empathy and a desire to provide entertainment for young children.

"welcomed them cheerily with reassuring smiles": this description of the staff confirms **the happy mood and atmosphere inside**.

Sentence Structure and Punctuation

"The local school was a drab old-fashioned building: the doors and windows were flaking paint; the stones of the walls were black with soot."
In this sentence, a **colon** introduces a **listing structure of sentences** separated by a **semicolon**. These sentences illustrate and emphasise the meaning of "drab".

"Yet, just as crusty human exteriors often disguise warm and kindly hearts, first impressions of this formidable structure belied the startling welcome inside: tiny tots who quavered through the massive doors on their first day found themselves surrounded by bright, rainbow-coloured walls and floors and doors; nursery rhyme characters were depicted on every available space; toys and games and cuddly toys were stacked round every corner."
 This **balanced sentence** emphasises the contrast between the bleak exterior and the happy interior of the building.
"crusty human exterior" balances with "first impressions of this formidable structure"
"warm and kindly hearts" balances with "startling welcome inside"

The **colon** introduces a **polysyndetic listing structure:**
"bright, rainbow-coloured walls and floors and

doors". This emphasises the large number of items painted in cheerful colours.

"toys and games and cuddly toys were stacked": the **polysyndetic listing** emphasises the large number of toys available for the children.

The **repetition** of "every" emphasises that there were many toys throughout the interior.

Linkage

"Yet, just as crusty human exteriors often disguise warm and kindly hearts, first impressions of this formidable structure belied the startling welcome inside."

"Yet": introduces a contrasting idea.

"crusty human exteriors" and "formidable structure": these phrases link back to "bleak edifice" in first paragraph which highlighted the ugly cold exterior of the building.

"warm and kindly hearts" and "startling welcome inside": these phrases link forward to positive description of interior which follows.

Page 146: FEELING THE HEAT

The title is effective because it indicates that the main purpose of passage is to describe varied reactions to intolerable heat.

Imagery

"like a furnace in the sky": the **simile** introduces **theme of intense heat**: a furnace creates destructive heat.

"relentless roasting": **the alliteration** emphasises **metaphor** of destructive heat.

"wilting and withering": the **alliteration** emphasises **metaphor** of plants suffering and dying in difficult circumstances.

"from the blast": the **metaphor** of blast continues theme of destructive heat.

"a caravan of camels and desert tribesmen": these references **establish metaphor** of hostile desert heat.

"as in a mirage": **continues metaphor** of the desert; the hot rising air is creating false pictures.

"the nearest oasis": **continues desert metaphor**: the oasis provides relief from harsh conditions.

"swathes of empty golden sand": the **image** suggests traditional idea of hot desert landscape.

Word Choice

"intense": **suggests** a very strong effect.

"sheltering": this has **connotations** of escaping from danger and **develops theme** of difficult situation caused by extreme heat.

"in just one week": the time limit emphasises that they spent lots of money on cold drinks.

"shimmering": refers to hot air rising, making surroundings appear to quiver.

"siesta": refers to the traditional practice of resting during the hottest part of the day when it is too uncomfortable to work.

"sleepy silence": **develops the idea** of siesta- people resting during hottest part of the day

"haze": refers to the misty effect of hot air rising and

distorting what we see.

"basic instincts of survival": has **connotations** of struggle in difficult circumstances and **develops theme** of unpleasant heat.

Irony

"sterner stuff": by the end of the passage this claim (that author was stronger than others) is contradicted; the irony is self-deprecating.

"(iced)": the parenthesis highlights ironic reference to earlier comment about weaker people buying a lot of cold drinks: it continues the tone of self-mockery.

Structure

The author **ends as she began** with references to dependence on cold drinks. Her earlier **derisory tone** and comments about weaker members of the party are **echoed** in the phrase "instincts of survival" and, **in parenthesis,** "iced". This echo emphasises that she also succumbed to the heat. In this way the irony emphatically sums up the main idea that the heat was unbearable.

Page 148: BULLYING

Main Purpose

This passage condemns the claim that we are dealing successfully with bullying throughout our society; it argues in favour of zero tolerance.

Word Choice

"apparent concern": implies that author doubts whether concern is genuine.

"subjugation by torment": the connotations of violence and suffering create a critical tone.

"much vaunted": suggests boasting and develops writer's critical tone.

"less desirable effects": suggests that bullying may be a result of such behaviour.

"superficial glance": suggests that people are not paying full attention so they have a false impression that bullying is being confronted successfully.

"might suggest" and "might claim": the use of the subjunctive creates uncertainty; it suggests that the claim that bullying is being dealt with effectively is not based on fact.

"outrageous and impossible suggestion": this is a derogatory description of the strategy for dealing with bullying.

"misguided": this is another critical reference to the official method of dealing with bullying.

"reduced to a shivering, nervous jelly of apprehension": this metaphor emphasises the negative effects of bullying: loss of confidence and nervousness.

Sentence Structure

"the subjugation by torment of one person by another": the parenthesis emphasises the definition of the unpleasant nature of bullying.

"determination, conviction and ruthless decisiveness": the listing structure highlights qualities often associated with success and admiration.

Minor Sentences

"Simple condemnation?": the repetition of official attitude presented in media is ironic and creates an incredulous, derogatory tone.

"What?: the single word, single syllable question emphasises her disbelief and tone of contempt.

"Zero tolerance?: the repetition of the official claim is ironic and mocking. "Absolutely": this one word sentence creates an emphatic, triumphant conclusion; it mocks failure of official strategy, compared to author's personal decisiveness.

Linkage

Paragraph 3: "however" indicates that there is a move away from acceptance of bullying; "nowadays" indicates the change of attitude is associated with time.

Paragraph 4: "Simple condemnation? Nothing could be further…" This repeats "simple condemnation" from the previous paragraph and creates mocking tone; it introduces an anecdote to illustrate author's contempt for official policy.

Conclusion

The author includes more mocking repetition of official policy; her ironic reference to "zero tolerance" emphasises her belief that only her solution works; the ironic repetition of "conviction and ruthless decisiveness" mocks the values mentioned at beginning of passage and thus emphasises the author's condemnation of bullying and the national failure to deal with it decisively.

Punctuation

Inverted commas round "character building" distance writer from this belief; she does not agree that such public school values are desirable.

"zero tolerance": the use of inverted commas emphasises that this expression is used by only some people and strongly suggests that the author does not agree with their opinion. In this way the punctuation highlights her mocking, incredulous tone.

Page 150: HOUSE ON THE HILL

This passage gives a vivid account of childhood memories.

Consider how the writer creates a vivid impression of the children's curiosity with word choice, sentence structure and punctuation in paragraph 1.

Word Choice

fascinated: means thrilled and gripped by something or someone of interest.

teased and tantalised: alliteration emphasises connotations of children being excited and driven to find out more.

drawn relentlessly: suggests non-stop overpowering urge to find out more about the house.

peered: connotations of struggling to see more

guessed wildly: connotations of great excitement and curiosity.

Sentence Structure and Punctuation

"They teased and tantalised our curiosity; we were drawn relentlessly; we peered and guessed wildly."

The listing structure highlights the strong attraction of the house and the children's need to find out more. Semi-colons emphasise that each sentence is about another aspect of their curiosity.

Comment on the effectiveness of linkage between paragraphs 2 and 3.

Paragraph Two: "deep jungle of rhododendron" begins to focus on a particularly wild part of estate. Paragraph Three: "dark enticing wilderness" echoes idea of untamed vegetation blocking out light.

In paragraph 3, how does the writer's use of language develop the idea of wilderness?

Word Choice

"mangled": suggests bush has grown out of control.

"a massive dome of thick glossy greenery": "massive"
and "thick" suggest great size and uncontrolled growth.
"impenetrable": suggests vegetation is so wild and
thick there is no way through.

Imagery

"vast tentacles of mangled rhododendron spread in a
wide circle": the metaphor of "tentacles" highlights
the length and spread of low branches.
"wriggling, scrabbling desperately secret route to the
centre": the transferred adjectives (epithets)
emphasise the thickness of vegetation and difficulty
of crawling through it.

**Consider how the author develops the idea, in
paragraph 4, that all the villagers saw the house
as an important feature of their lives.**

The house had been renamed by the villagers.
New name was personified to represent whole family.
Listing structure offers examples of personification:
"the 'house on the hill' had gone for the summer; it
had left for an important wedding in London; it was
clearly expecting important visitors."

**In paragraphs 5 and 6, how does the writer
develop the importance of the "house on the hill"?**

Mr Hinchley's respect and awe:

"bristling with urgency" suggests tension/ anxiety.
"flourished" indicates the importance of list to him.
"barked": onomatopoeia suggests urgency and
tension.

Customers' acceptance that they are less
important:
"abandoned"
"quietly step aside in awe"

Assistants' eagerness to help:
"scurried" suggests they were rushing about.
"anxiously" suggests tension.
"distracted by the demands of perfect service"
explains cause of tension was the importance of order
from the House on the Hill.

In paragraph 7 what techniques does the writer
use to indicate that a great deal of time has
passed since his childhood?

Parenthesis
"a lifetime later": establishes that a long time has
passed.

Repetition

"so important...so marvellous... were still there":
emphasises relief- suggests long gap of time created
uncertainty.

Listing Structure

"so much that had happened, so many adventures, so much happiness, so many dearly loved friends": highlights great number of events and people and suggests a large space of time.

Pluperfect Tense

"so much that had happened" indicates that all these things happened before this visit.

Ellipsis (three dots): indicates that there is much more to be said about the time that has passed.

Page 153: OIL ON GRANITE

The central concern of this passage is the author's admiration of two aspects of the city of Aberdeen: the complexity and huge size of the oil industry and the strength of the traditional culture of the city. She argues that the old city copes very well with the arrival of the oil industry.

1. In paragraph 1, comment on the effectiveness of the sentence structure in sentences 2 and 3.

- These sentences develop the positive tone introduced with "marvellous".
- They have identical structures: negative to positive.

- The negatives are "not big" and "asleep".
- In both sentences these negatives are developed in parenthesis.
- Each sentence changes from negative to positive at "but".
- The positives are "always in motion" and "brilliantly awake".

2.   How does the writer develop the idea of the harbour being "brilliantly awake"?

- "brilliantly awake": suggests the harbour was brightly lit.
- "glitter": has connotations of sparkling light.
- "fireworks spray": the metaphor suggests lots of very colourful light around the welders.
- "shrouded shape": the contrasting darkness of this area emphasises the light in the harbour.

3.   In paragraph 2, by referring to the writer's use of language, show how she creates a vivid impression of noise and movement in the harbour.

- "hissing, clanging and thumping": the list of onomatopoeic present participles emphasises lots of noise and movement.
- "scud", "heaves" and "slips": these verbs suggest many sorts of boats are moving at different speeds.
- "clanking": another onomatopoeic present participle, adds to sense of noise and movement.

- "exchanging Scotticisms": suggests that there is a lot of shouting.

4. In paragraph 3, with particular reference to sentence structure, show how the writer develops her point that Aberdeen is the centre of the North Sea Oil industry.

- "chief support base": suggests Aberdeen is main source of activity.
- "supply ships…depots": the listing structure of equipment and transport emphasises huge scale of activity.
- "Here": placed at the beginning of an inverted sentence structure, this word emphasises the importance of Aberdeen.
- Last sentence contains a list of 3 sentences about key aspects of huge industry (money, international skills and varied nationalities of people in the industry).
- "through this conduit" and repetition of "here" emphasise that everything comes to Aberdeen.
- "Americans, Englishmen…Germans": the listing structure of nationalities represented in Aberdeen suggests a massive international operation.

5. In paragraph 4, show how the writer indicates a change of theme.

- "Yet" suggests change of direction.
- change of time and light: "as night falls".

- "grave and grey": the connotations of stillness and seriousness are highlighted by alliteration and assonance.

6. In the same paragraph, by referring to word choice, sentence structure and imagery, show how she makes it clear that Aberdeen has reacted very cautiously to the arrival of the oil industry.

- "like keepers of the public conscience": simile with "conscience" suggests a very serious attitude.
- "sentinel" means guard: suggests caution.
- "no skyscrapers, revolving restaurants on towers, neon lights or blazing late-night stores": negative listing structure emphasises lack of excitement.
- "hardly more than a backdrop to the performance": theatre imagery suggests Aberdeen is standing back from the excitement of oil industry.
- "old and respected burgh": word choice emphasises great age and serious reputation of Aberdeen; the contrast with excitement of "boom towns" emphasises seriousness.
- "tentative to the experience": word choice continues idea of caution and seriousness.
- "Other towns have gold rushes or silver strikes: Aberdeen's is a strictly granite bonanza.": the balanced sentence structure sets "Other towns" against "Aberdeen's" and highlights Aberdeen's cautious reaction to oil industry. "Gold" and "silver" have connotations of showy wealth which contrasts with plain, heavy nature of "granite".

7.   Comment on the effectiveness of the link between paragraph 4 and paragraph 5.

- "Handsome, civilised, diligent, granite": the list of adjectives ends in "granite" which echoes "granite" at end of paragraph 4.
- "has never been rich before, but has always been canny": the change from negative "never been rich" to positive "always been canny" continues theme of caution.

8.   Which aspect of Aberdeen does the writer introduce in paragraph 5 as a symbol of the fact that Aberdeen has not changed much throughout history?

- unchanging buildings/ architecture

9.   In paragraph 6, how does the writer develop her use of this symbol- making it a vehicle for her argument that Aberdeen has strong traditions?

- "very hard to date a building": buildings have not changed with time. This suggests Aberdeen keeps its traditions.
- "severe granite villas": repetition of "granite" continues idea of great age and seriousness.
- "scarcely ostentatious": word choice of "ostentatious" continues idea that Aberdeen does not get excited by change; it does not show off.

- "Footdee... still occupied by fishing families": word choice of "still" suggests Aberdeen people do not change or move easily.

10. In paragraph 7, how does the writer develop her theme of tradition?

- repeated sentence structure places "here" at the beginning of 2 sentences. This emphasises Aberdeen's importance to the traditional industries.
- "traditionally": word choice emphasises the long history of existing fish and farming industries.
- "deeply rooted" has connotations of firm traditions that will not change easily.

11. In paragraph 8, which part of Aberdeen does the writer now use to develop the idea of tradition?

The Auction Mart

12. By discussing her use of language show how the writer creates a vivid sense of place in this paragraph.

- "little has really changed": continues idea of tradition.
- "each morning": word choice of "each" has connotations of regularity and reliability.
- "timeless, stalwart, comely men, their faces rigid in the truest Scottish mould, unhurried, polite": the listing structure of adjectives gives vivid

impression of fishermen and continues idea of history and tradition.

- "timeless": word choice suggests these men have been the same for a very long time.

- "the truest Scottish mould": the metaphor suggests that they have had the same appearance for generations.

- "as they always did": continues idea of tradition in this part of Aberdeen.

- "the slithering of seaboots, the clattering of boxes, the chugging of engines, the shrieking of seabirds, the slurping of tea from enamel mugs": listing structure of onomatopoeic present participles creates vivid impression of business and noise.

- "immemorially": means "beyond memory"; word choice continues idea of long history at the mart and people still behaving in the same way.

13. In paragraph 9, comment on the effect of the writer's use of the words "exhilarating", "exuberance" and "fizzy". How do they contribute to the overall argument of the passage?

- "Exhilarating" means uplifting and exciting: the word choice is associated with the usual excitement of oil booms which Aberdeen has avoided.

- "Exuberance" has connotations of energy and excitement- avoided by traditional Aberdeen.

- "fizzy" means bubbly and has connotations of energy and lots of activity. This is what old Aberdeen has avoided so far.

- Repetition of "not" emphasises that Aberdeen is avoiding these things.
- The passage contrasts excitement of "oil" with seriousness of traditional Aberdeen, symbolised by granite: this paragraph emphasises that contrast.

14. Why has she written fizzy in italics?

Italics indicate that this is a quotation: she has interviewed a local person. Quotations demonstrate veracity of report: the journalist has researched the subject by visiting the areas.

15. In paragraph 10 show how the writer has used sentence structure, word choice and other techniques to make her meaning clear.

- The whole paragraph is climactic- ending in "best of all possible burghs".
- The purpose of paragraph is to praise the existing city- separate from the oil industry.
- The listing structure of features linked to superlative "lowest" is polysyndetic which emphasises the admiring tone.
- The superlative adjective "highest" is also part of a polysyndetic list which emphasises positive features of Aberdeen.
- "tastefully" and "discreetly" have connotations of good judgement which echo previous references to the fact that Aberdeen is a serious, long-established city. This idea is symbolised by "granite".

16. In paragraph 11, with reference to word choice and other language techniques, show how the author brings her two main ideas together.

The two key themes are, firstly, the traditional old city of Aberdeen and, secondly, the energy and excitement of the oil industry.

- "fallen more or less out of the sky": this metaphor emphasises the sudden shock of arrival of oil industry and brings two themes together: it reflects title of article.

- "hoary and provident": this phrase sums up first theme of tradition and caution: "hoary" means whitehaired and old; "provident" suggests careful wisdom.

- "bonanza" suggests wild riches, feasting and celebrations: sums up the description of oil industry.

- "seen against so stolid a setting, it is staggering": alliteration emphasises contrast between the key words "stolid" and "staggering".

- staggering" has connotations of shock at huge impact of oil industry.

- "stolid" suggests slowness; it echoes description of Aberdeen as a serious city with slow and careful response to oil industry.

- "mere million", "billion or two" and "nothing modest" develop the theme of huge size and shock of arrival of oil industry.

17. In paragraph 12, by discussing the writer's use of imagery and other language techniques, show how she emphasises the huge impact of the oil industry on Aberdeen.

- "like a war": the simile of war is effective; it emphasises the great size and complicated nature of the oil industry with massive resources and huge numbers of people.
- "like a rollcall of regiments, drawn from all corners of some great alliance and assembled beneath their several flags": this simile echoes the description of the huge size and international nature of oil industry in paragraph 3.
- "billeted": refers to enforced accommodation of staff by local communities in wartime.
- "officers of some occupying army" emphasises strangeness of oil industry to Aberdeen.
- "staffs and technical corps of the campaign" suggests huge numbers of people.
- "intelligence base" suggests complicated nature of industry.

18. With reference to the writer's central concern, her two contrasting themes and her use of language techniques, show how paragraph 13 is an effective conclusion to this article.

- "beauty here", "beauty of power and innovation": repeated references to beauty are now applied to oil industry.

- Alliteration and juxtaposition of "brutal beauty" highlight the idea that oil industry can be beautiful, like old Aberdeen.
- These references to beauty echo description of the beauty of old Aberdeen in paragraph 8.
- "hard northern coastline, where the wild storms sweep in from the sea" and "clippers sailed out to capture the prizes": the description of old Aberdeen is now more aggressive with references to violent weather and the determined clippers.
- The writer brings two themes together by arguing finally that the oil industry and old Aberdeen are both beautiful and both understand the tough world of enterprise.

- The final sentence is balanced: "may have their doubts" balances against "can hardly quarrel"; "London even about Edinburgh" balances against "Aberdeen". This brings article to a firm conclusion that, despite their differences, Aberdeen and oil industry get on well together.

Printed in Great Britain
by Amazon